MONEYWORK

Moneywork

FUEL YOUR FREEDOM WITH DIVIDEND INCOME

PAUL L. DURSO

HOUNDSTOOTH
PRESS

MONEYWORK
Fuel Your Freedom with Dividend Income

FIRST EDITION

ISBN 978-1-5445-5093-0 *Hardcover*
978-1-5445-5092-3 *Paperback*
978-1-5445-5094-7 *Ebook*

To my clients—past, present, and the brave souls who haven't met me yet.

Thank you for trusting me with your dreams, your dollars, and occasionally your panic-emailed GIFs of burning stock charts. You've taught me more than any finance textbook: that patience beats headlines, panic is temporary, and late-night snacks are a legitimate asset class.

May your dividends grow faster than your grandkids. May your portfolios compound like laundry in a teenager's room. May you always remember that "sleep-well money" is the best currency on earth.

Here's to the paychecks your portfolios will keep sending long after we're all debating whether robots can reinvest for us. This book—and every quarterly deposit—belongs to you.

Contents

INTRODUCTION

From Hot Tub to Headfirst

My Journey into Dividend Investing

The sun was setting over the Pacific, casting that perfect golden glow that made everything feel cinematic. San Diego was buzzing. I was there for a financial conference, surrounded by some of the sharpest minds in the industry. But the moment that would forever change my approach to investing wasn't happening in one of the crowded conference rooms. Nope, the event unfolded in a hot tub.

There we were, financial advisors from across the country, unwinding after a long day of sessions. As steam rose around us, we did what financial folks do: talked markets, discussed strategies, and swapped stories about the latest investment trends. Everyone, myself included, believed they understood the investing world well.

And then it happened. One of my advisor friends, a guy I'd always respected for his deep understanding of the markets, casually dropped a comment that made me stop and listen: "Dividends are the unsung heroes of investing. Most people don't truly understand their power."

I nodded along, pretending to keep up, but inside I felt a knot of embarrassment tighten. Here I was, deep into my career as a financial advisor, yet I knew almost nothing about dividend investing. I thought dividends were just little bonuses—extra cash companies paid out if things went well. I had no idea there was so much more to the dividend stock story.

As my friend peeled back the layers, explaining how dividends provided stability in volatile markets, how companies with a strong dividend culture would protect those payouts, even during tough times, it was like a fog lifted. He talked about how companies would do anything, even cut jobs, before they cut dividends. He explained that high-yield stocks could be traps, like fool's gold, tempting but dangerous if you didn't know how to spot the ones built on shaky foundations.

By the time I climbed out of that hot tub, my mind was buzzing with ideas. That night, I stayed up late researching everything I could about dividend investing. The seed was planted, but I wasn't fully invested yet (pun intended). The spark had ignited, but the passion? That would come later, as I continued down this path.

THE TURNING POINT: BUILDING SIMPLICITREE AND SEEING THE POWER OF DIVIDENDS

Fast-forward a few years. I was in the early stages of building what would later become Simplicitree, our income planning software. At first, it was just a rough concept in an Excel spreadsheet, a stark contrast to the powerful software it has evolved into. But even in those early days, something amazing happened.

As I built out the platform and began testing different income strategies, one thing kept standing out: dividend investing. No matter what strategy we threw at a client's income shortfall, whether it involved bonds, annuities, or capital-gains-focused portfolios, dividend-growth investing became the solution that often solved the problem. Not just sometimes but almost every time.

Then it clicked like that moment in a suspense movie where the alien touches the mind of a human and all wisdom comes flooding in. I remembered the hot tub conversation, the late-night research, and just about every aspect of dividend investing I had learned poured into my mind at one moment. I made a commitment to learn everything about dividend investing, and the inevitable happened next.

I decided to go all in on dividends. I am not that guy who learns something new and says, "Eh, I'll unpack that later." No, once I saw the power of dividend-growth investing, I dove in headfirst. I hired some of the best dividend managers I could find, and they taught me everything they knew, for a price. The price I paid was the best investment I've ever made. I absorbed it all. Then, after years of managing assets with outside help, I took the reins and began managing my clients' portfolios as the asset manager.

BEEN THERE, DONE THAT: THE SEARCH FOR THE PERFECT STRATEGY

Here's the thing: I wasn't always convinced of the power of dividend investing. In fact, throughout my career, I have tried just about every investment strategy you can think of. You name it, I've hired someone to manage it or tested it out myself. Mutual funds, ETFs, indexes, market timing—you could say I've been around the block a few times. I've hired some of the best strategists in the business, working with big institutions, chasing the latest and greatest trends, hoping to find that elusive, perfect strategy.

And do you know what all those strategies had in common? Continual disappointment and frustration. Over and over, I saw the same result: They didn't work as promised. The returns were underwhelming, the risks were too high, or the outcomes were too inconsistent to rely on for long-term financial security.

This endless cycle of disappointment is something I see investors go through all the time. They bounce from advisor to advisor, chasing the next big strategy that will supposedly change their financial future. But most of those strategies are built on shaky ground—designed to impress in the short term but lacking the long-term staying power that investors really need.

Which brings me back to dividends. Unlike all those flashy strategies that come and go, dividend-growth investing has stood the test of time. It wasn't a get-rich-quick scheme. It was a steady, reliable way to build wealth over the long haul. The more I dug into it, the more I realized it wasn't just *a* solution—it was *the* solution. As I continued to build Simplicitree and stress-test every scenario, dividends kept coming out on top. Over the long term, value investing—and specifically dividend-growth investing—beats growth strategies almost every time. In fact, as you'll see in the next chapter, when you zoom out far enough, value always wins.

WHY THIS BOOK? WHY NOW?

Here I am, decades into my career, sharing everything I've learned with you. I packed this book with the secrets and strategies I've discovered through years of trial, error, and finally, success. I'm passionate about this because I've seen how powerful dividend-growth investing can be—both for my clients and for my personal portfolio. The crazy thing is, you don't need me or any financial advisor to do this. You can apply everything in this book on your own.

My clients always tell me, "Paul, we want to learn everything you know," and I'm happy to share it. I tell them that I want them to understand these strategies so well that if something ever happened to me, they could carry on without missing a beat. And yet, they still want me in their lives. Why? Because even though they *can* do this alone, they don't want to find themselves in a situation where they don't know what to do, so they keep me around. We are a dream team for their financial future. They dream it up, and we figure it out together!

The ultimate goal of the book is to empower you with the tools, knowledge, and confidence to build an income strategy that's not only sustainable but also perfectly suited to your unique financial journey. From understanding your shortfall to strategically using what you've learned about dividend-growth investing, I want you to walk away with enough insight to create an income plan that provides peace of mind and the financial freedom you've been working toward.

As you read this book, know that you're getting decades of experience distilled into these pages. I've been there, done that, and learned what works. Now, I'm handing you the playbook.

You're about to learn the secrets the industry doesn't want you to know, the strategies that have stood the test of time, and most importantly, how to keep yourself in control of your most dangerous enemy: your emotions.

Are you ready?

WE'LL START WITH THE GREAT DEBATE: VALUE VERSUS GROWTH INVESTING

We'll begin with one of the longest-running debates in the investing world: value versus growth. It's like the eternal argument of "Who's the greatest?" Is it Jordan, LeBron, or Kobe? In the investing world, it's growth stocks with their flashy, short-term gains versus value stocks built for long-term success.

You're going to see why growth stocks can make headlines but often disappoint over time, while value stocks—slow, steady, and often overlooked—quietly win the race. We'll talk about why value investing dominates in the long run, and I'll share some stories from my career where clients learned this lesson the hard way (and how they bounced back).

If you've ever wondered which strategy is right for you, this chapter will finally settle the debate. Spoiler alert: Value wins every time over the long haul, and I'm going to show you why.

Get ready to challenge everything you've thought about "what's hot" in the market, because we're about to break down why boring is beautiful when it comes to building long-term wealth!

CHAPTER 1

Settling the Great Debate: Value Versus Growth Investing

The Tortoise, the Hare, and the Hidden MVP

Have you picked a side yet? I wrestle with it every time I pull on an old NBA jersey. As a kid, I'd sprawl on the living-room carpet—popcorn, check...rabbit-ear TV, check—and watch Michael Jordan hang in midair like gravity had asked for his autograph. In college, my roommates and I stayed up past midnight yelling "KOBE!" whenever a wadded-up Taco Bell wrapper found the trash can. And now my wife just shakes her head while I cue up YouTube so the kids can witness LeBron whip a no-look, laser-beam pass through four defenders as if he's playing 4D chess in size fifteen sneakers.

Jordan? Six rings, five MVPs, ten scoring titles, and that ice-cold "give me the ball and-get out of the way" instinct that broke more hearts than a season finale of *The Bachelor*. Kobe? The Black Mamba—five championships, an eighty-one-point night that still sounds like a clerical error, and a work ethic that made alarm clocks nervous. LeBron? Part power forward, part point guard—top-five in both career points *and* assists, a chase-down-block highlight reel, and the durability to put up All-NBA numbers long after most stars are shopping for golf carts.

The catch? They never played by the same rules, schedules, or eras. "Greatest of All Time" really boils down to which highlight tape you cue up and which stat column you circle in red ink.

In my day job, there's a debate just as fierce and far more likely to hijack client meetings than barstool banter: value versus growth investing. And just like the GOAT argument, declaring a winner without context can leave you shouting at the TV—or worse, at your brokerage account—for years.

GROWTH STOCKS: THE FLASHY WINNER?

Growth stocks are the LeBrons of the investing world: exciting, high-flying, and able to generate eye-popping returns in the short term. Tech companies are often the poster children for growth stocks. You know the types: Amazon, Tesla, Google, and Apple, all riding waves of innovation and demand.

Growth stocks, like LeBron's monster dunks, grab your attention and get people talking. They're the ones you see making headlines with huge gains—doubling or tripling in a matter of years, sometimes months. During market booms, like the one we saw in the 2010s tech bull run, growth stocks outshine everything else. If you're purely focused on quick returns or riding market sentiment, it's hard not to fall for growth stocks.

Here's where it gets interesting.

THE LONG GAME: VALUE INVESTING IS A TIMELESS CHAMPION

On the other side of the debate, we've got value stocks. They're the Michael Jordans of investing. At first glance, they might not turn heads. Value stocks don't have the flashy allure of the tech-driven growth sector, but once you zoom out and look at the bigger picture, you realize they always win. Value stocks represent companies that are *undervalued* relative to their intrinsic worth. These companies might not be in the trendiest sectors—think healthcare, financials, or energy—but they have rock-solid fundamentals, steady free cash flow, and a long track record of performance. They're not in it for short-term fame; they're here for long-term dominance.

Now, let's dig into the numbers to settle this debate. Historically, value stocks have significantly outperformed growth stocks when measured over a long enough time horizon. According to data from 1927 onward, value stocks have delivered an average annual return of 11.5 percent, while growth stocks have managed 7.1 percent.[1] That's a 4.4 percent annual difference, which might not seem monumental at first, but when compounded over decades, the gap becomes staggering.

I'll break that down with an example. If you had invested $10,000 in value stocks and another $10,000 in growth stocks back in 1927, your value stock portfolio today would be worth several million dollars more than the growth stock portfolio. The difference? Over time, value stocks benefit from the power of compounding returns. Value investing doesn't just sprint ahead for quick wins—it dominates the marathon.

Several factors drive these superior returns. Value stocks are often undervalued relative to their earnings, meaning investors buy them at a discount. Over time, the market wakes up, realizes the bargain,

---

1 "Current Research Returns," Kenneth R. French—Data Library, accessed October 21, 2025, https://mba.tuck.dartmouth.edu/pages/faculty/ken.french/data_library.html.

and the price catches up, so value stocks rise. Combine that with dividends—and many value stocks offer consistent payouts that growth stocks skip—and you get a long-term winning formula. It's a steady, predictable path to wealth, in contrast to the sometimes volatile nature of growth investing.

So, when you're looking at the long game, value investing doesn't just keep pace with growth; it surpasses it by a wide margin. Like Jordan, value stocks may not dominate every single game, but when you look back at the *career*, there's no denying who the true champion is.

I know what you're thinking: "Great! If I were a 110-year-old vampire, I'd be thrilled with a 1927 starting date, but I need my money working *this* side of the century mark." Fair point. So let's shrink the timeline to something that fits inside a normal career.

Picture New Year's Day 2000—Y2K bunker kits on clearance, dial-up tones still echoing through the house. You drop $10,000 into a broad US value index and another $10,000 into a comparable growth index, then do the hardest thing in investing: nothing. Fast-forward just twenty years to the end of 2019—a period that includes the dot-com bust, 9/11, the Great Financial Crisis, and more market mood swings than a toddler at bedtime. Your growth stake limps across the finish line at roughly $33,000. Respectable. But your value stake? It's sitting at about $41,000—almost 25 percent more—*plus* you collected fatter dividend checks the whole way.[2]

In other words, you didn't need a century to watch value fundamentals, and those relentless dividend payments, do their Michael Jordan thing. Two decades—one working lifetime, one retirement glide path—was enough to turn the tortoise into the clear winner.

2 "Current Research Returns," Kenneth R. French—Data Library.

BUILDING THE CASE: WHEN VALUE TAKES OVER

Now, if you take a bunch of shorter time frames—like a few years here and there—growth often looks like it's winning. The 1990s tech boom and the post-2008 financial crisis era saw growth stocks explode. However, like Jordan's legacy, which is defined not by a single game but by his *whole career*, the long view reveals value investing's true greatness.

Historically, value stocks outperform growth stocks after periods of excessive speculation. Remember the dot-com bubble in the early 2000s? Growth stocks, in the tech sector, were the talk of the town, much like LeBron in his early Cleveland days. But when the bubble burst, value stocks, grounded in strong fundamentals, took over and dominated the 2000s.[3]

It's the same story after the 2008 financial crisis. Growth stocks recovered quickly, but value stocks were the ones quietly building wealth, paying dividends, and offering stability.

THE INFLECTION POINT: HOW LONG DOES IT TAKE?

Now, you might ask, "How long does it take value stocks to prove their superiority?" Research suggests that after ten to fifteen years, value stocks almost always outperform growth stocks. Over shorter periods, growth can dominate, particularly during speculative market phases or industry-specific booms. But if you zoom out to twenty years or more, value comes out on top. It's like watching Jordan's six championships unfold over time—the longer you watch, the more obvious his dominance becomes.

---

3 Brandon Bischof, "Value vs. Growth: A Brief Historical View," Nasdaq, May 6, 2021, https://www.nasdaq.com/articles/value-vs-growth%3A-a-brief-historical-view-2021-05-06.

WHY VALUE WORKS: THE LONG-TERM FORMULA

So, why does value investing work so well in the long run? It comes down to a few key factors:

1. **Strong Fundamentals:** Value stocks typically have better price-to-earnings ratios, higher dividend yields, and solid cash flows. They're companies that make sense on paper, and they're often undervalued by the market because they're not in the "hot" industries.
2. **Dividends:** Value stocks often pay dividends, which, when reinvested, compound over time. That steady income stream helps build wealth through the ups and downs of the market.
3. **Mean Reversion:** Markets are cyclical. After a period of excessive growth, stock prices typically revert back to their mean, which gives value stocks a natural advantage when growth stocks fall out of favor.

In contrast, growth stocks often rely on high expectations and future promises, which can lead to inflated prices and disappointment if those expectations aren't met. When growth stocks fall, they often fall hard. Just look at Amazon in the early 2000s or Tesla after any earnings miss.

THE ANSWER: VALUE TAKES THE CROWN

After all the back and forth, here's the answer: value investing wins the long game. Yes, growth stocks might have their moments of brilliance, just like LeBron might have a game where he drops fifty points. But if you want to build long-term wealth, value stocks are your best bet. They're steady, they're reliable, and when you stretch the timeline out long enough, they always outperform growth.

THE PROOF IS IN THE PORTFOLIO

I had a client named Mike who treated his brokerage app like a slot machine. Every other call was, "Paul, ABC stock up 18 percent this week—why don't we own more?" The highs were intoxicating…right until the inevitable 25 percent plunge had him emailing me at 2:00 a.m. "Should we bail before things get worse?" Mike didn't need a financial plan; he needed antacids.

After one too many "up big, down bigger" cycles, he finally sighed and said, "Forget the excitement. I need a paycheck I can sleep on." We rebuilt his portfolio around rock-solid, dividend-growing companies. Ten years later, the numbers told the story: His old "thrill ride" growth picks would've netted roughly 110 percent total return and a lot of Tylenol. His new dividend lineup: 180 percent total return **plus** a quarterly income stream that kept showing up whether the market was celebrating or sulking.

Mike still checks his app, but now it's to see how much cash hit his account, not whether his portfolio survived the latest roller-coaster drop. That's the difference between chasing excitement and owning reliability.

GO FOR THE LONG GAME

Investing is about building wealth over time, not getting rich quick. The growth versus value debate has been going on for decades, but when you step back and take a broader view, the answer becomes very clear.

Value stocks are like the Jordan of investing: consistent, dominant, and unbeatable when you look at the full career. Growth stocks may give you a thrill, but value stocks will help you cross the finish line.

So, when the market tries to distract you with the latest shiny growth stock, just remember: Jordan didn't win six championships by chasing highlights. He won by mastering the fundamentals and playing the long game. And in investing, value stocks are your way to play that long game.

Wait…what about Kobe? Did I just forget him? Don't worry, I'm saving Black Mamba for later.

THE POWER OF DIVIDENDS AND PATIENCE

You've just tackled one of the biggest debates in investing—value versus growth—and hopefully, you've come away seeing the long-term dominance of value investing.

Next, let's dive into a new challenge: benchmarks. We'll explore why chasing popular benchmarks like the S&P 500 and NASDAQ could actually be holding you back. Think of it like comparing your life to someone's Instagram feed—it's a curated, sometimes misleading version of success. I'll show you why these common benchmarks aren't the gold standard they're made out to be, and more importantly, how you can craft your own personal benchmark that truly reflects your financial goals.

CHAPTER 2

Benching the Benchmarks

Why Following the Crowd Could Sideline Your Success

"If all your friends jumped off a cliff, would you do it too?" My mom's favorite rhetorical question always popped up whenever I came home with a new bruise or a questionable haircut. As a kid, I never quite grasped the profundity behind it. I mean, of course I wouldn't jump off a cliff—unless there was a cool trampoline at the bottom or I was connected to a bungee cord. As I grew older, I realized Mom wasn't just trying to save me from physical harm or fashion disasters; she was teaching me the importance of forging my own path.

If you don't mind, I'd like to share a personal story to this effect, and then get into benchmarks.

KNOWING THE RIGHT LEADER FROM THE WRONG: A NIGHT OF MISCHIEF AND A MOMENT OF TRUTH

One crisp fall evening during my high school years, my family had relatives visiting from out of town. The house was bustling, and amid the chaos, I invited a friend over—let's call him Johnny. Now Johnny wasn't exactly the poster child for good decisions, but he was fun, and at that age, that's all that mattered.

As night fell and everyone else drifted off to sleep, Johnny had an idea. "Let's go out and have some fun," he whispered. Caught up in the thrill of rebellion, I agreed. We gathered our covert supplies—eggs, toilet paper, and some ladyfinger firecrackers—and slipped out into the cool night.

Our escapades began innocently enough, though while jumping off the back deck, we seemed to break our neighbor's picnic table (sorry, Mr. Wendle!). We tossed eggs at a couple of houses, decorated trees with toilet paper, and set off firecrackers in strategic locations to maximize the surprise. Feeling invincible, we also placed trash cans in precarious positions just to see what would happen. The adrenaline was intoxicating.

Emboldened by our success, we upped the ante. We strung together a bunch of ladyfinger firecrackers, placed each of them inside an egg, and set them off near the top of a car parked in our neighborhood. The sound exceeded our expectations. Laughing like the carefree teenagers we were, we retreated to a safe distance.

However, curiosity got the better of us. Later that night, we circled back to admire our handiwork. As we approached, the porch light flicked on, and the car's owner emerged, eyes scanning the darkness. "Hey! Stop right there!" he shouted. Panic surged through me. Johnny didn't hesitate. He bolted straight into the woods. I turned to run as well, but then something unexpected happened.

"Stop! Come back here!" the man called again.

For reasons I still can't fully explain, I halted. Maybe it was the tone of his voice, or a guilty feeling, that might have caused it. I took a deep breath, turned around, and walked toward him.

We stood on his front porch under the dim light, and the distant sounds of the night blanketed us.

"Why did you do this?" he asked, not angrily, but with genuine curiosity. "Do you know me? Was this some kind of personal vendetta?"

I shook my head. "No, sir. It was just a dumb decision. I'm really sorry."

We talked for about twenty-five minutes while waiting for the police to arrive—yes, he had called them. He asked about my family, my interests, and why a kid like me would make such a poor choice. I had no answers, just apologies.

Finally, he sighed and said, "You know what? Go home. Just promise me you'll come back tomorrow to clean up the mess."

I looked him in the eye and said, "Mr. Thompson, I made this decision, and I need to face the consequences. I'm not running from this."

To this day, I don't know why I stayed. Part of me wishes I'd taken his offer, but another part recognizes that this was a turning point in my life. The police arrived, and I had to face the uncomfortable ride home, explaining to my parents what had happened.

In the weeks that followed, I kept my promise. I cleaned Mr. Thompson's car. Fortunately for me, it involved only a lot of egg residue, but no damage to his car. Surprisingly, we became friends. He offered me advice, shared stories from his youth, and became something of a mentor. Meanwhile, Johnny continued on a different path, one that led us to drift apart.

That night, I went from being a carefree boy to taking the first steps toward becoming a responsible man. I learned the importance of owning my actions and not just going along with the crowd. It was a hard lesson but a valuable one, shaping who I am today.

THE MIRAGE OF MARKET BENCHMARKS

Fast-forward to today. You'll find plenty of investors who act like Johnny: sneaking out at night to cause mischief. Except they're not messing around in neighborhoods, but in their portfolios. They're following the allure of market benchmarks like the S&P 500 and the NASDAQ, often without understanding the potential consequences. People tout these indices as the gold standard for measuring investment success, but using them as your personal benchmark can lead you astray.

THE S&P 500: A NOT-SO-GOLDEN STANDARD

Let's start with the S&P 500. At first glance, it seems like a reasonable benchmark—it's made up of 500 of the largest companies in the US. But let's peel back the layers.

Cap-Weighting Woes

The S&P 500 is cap-weighted, meaning companies with larger market capitalizations have a greater impact on the index's performance. Market capitalization is calculated by multiplying a company's stock price by its total number of outstanding shares. This methodology heavily skews the index toward the biggest players.

As of 2023, the top twenty-five companies in the S&P 500—just 5 percent of the index—account for over 40 percent of its total market capitalization.[4] A tiny fraction of companies drive the performance of the entire index. If those top corporations have a bad day, so does the S&P 500. Conversely, the top corporations overshadow the performance of the other 475 companies.

---

4 S&P Dow Jones "S&P 500 Sector and Concentration Dashboard," February 2024.

Lack of Diversification

But wait, there's more! The S&P 500 isn't just top-heavy; it's also sector-heavy. The index is divided into eleven sectors, but the split is far from even.[5]

- **Information Technology:** About 27 percent
- **Healthcare:** Around 14 percent
- **Financials:** Close to 11 percent

Combine the top three sectors, and you're looking at over 50 percent of the index's weighting. To put this into perspective, there are more than 160 sectors in the US economy that are broken down by specific industry groups.[6] Yet the S&P 500 covers only eleven broad sectors, with just a few dominating the index. So much for diversification! If you're using the S&P 500 as your benchmark, you're essentially comparing your performance to a tech-heavy portfolio dominated by a handful of giants.

Here's the irony: The financial industry consistently tells us that diversification is essential. "Don't put all your eggs in one basket," they say. And yet, the very benchmarks we are handed—like the S&P 500 and NASDAQ—are far from diversified.

A handful of sectors and companies dominate these indices, creating a "do as I say, not as I do" contradiction. Why are we constantly told to diversify, but then measured against benchmarks that are anything but? It's a head-scratcher, and it leaves many investors chasing an unrealistic and skewed standard when true diversification would look quite different.

---

5 Same fact sheet (Table 2).

6 S&P Dow Jones Indices, *Global Industry Classification Standard (GICS): Methodology* (October 2024), page 4, https://www.spglobal.com/spdji/en/documents/methodologies/methodology-gics.pdf.

THE NASDAQ: TECH TITAN OR ONE-TRICK PONY?

Then there's the NASDAQ Composite, which is even more concentrated. Unlike the NASDAQ 100, which focuses on the largest nonfinancial companies, the NASDAQ Composite includes more than 3,500 companies. Impressive diversity, right? Not so fast.

The Illusion of Variety

Despite boasting thousands of companies, the NASDAQ Composite isn't as diverse as it appears. It's cap-weighted, just like the S&P 500, meaning the larger the company, the more influence it has on the index's performance. The top fifty companies alone make up over 60 percent of the index's total market capitalization.[7] That means the performance of just 1.4 percent of the companies dictates the overall fate of the NASDAQ Composite.

To put that into perspective, imagine you have a giant pitcher of water, representing the entire NASDAQ Composite with its 3,500 companies. Now, take a small drop of highly concentrated food coloring and drop it into the pitcher. Even though it's just one drop, that tiny amount changes the color of the entire pitcher. The same thing happens with the NASDAQ Composite. Just like that single drop of color can dominate a large volume of water, the performance of a small group of companies dramatically influences the direction of the whole index. Despite having thousands of companies in the mix, the fate of the index hinges on a tiny percentage.

Sector Saturation

The NASDAQ is predominantly technology-focused. If you're benchmarking against the NASDAQ, you're essentially comparing your

---

7 Nasdaq "Indexology" blog, 2024-09-12 post "Concentration in the Composite."

portfolio to one that is heavily concentrated in tech companies. Unless technology stocks also dominate your portfolio, this comparison is not just unbalanced—it's irrelevant. It's like comparing apples to oranges—or in this case, Apple to everything else. The two simply don't align, and using the NASDAQ as a benchmark for a diversified portfolio will almost always lead to misleading conclusions.

THE BENCHMARK BLUES: WHY THIS MATTERS TO YOU

So, why shouldn't you measure your portfolio against these widely accepted benchmarks? The following are a few reasons.

Chasing Unicorns

Unless you own a significant chunk of the top companies dominating these indices, you're unlikely to match their performance. This can lead to unnecessary stress and the false belief that your investment strategy is failing. But here's the thing: Not matching the benchmarks isn't a bad outcome. While everyone dreams of keeping pace with the market when it's soaring, no one wants to mirror those same benchmarks when they take a nosedive.

Indexes like the NASDAQ and S&P 500 are notoriously volatile. They can skyrocket in good times but plummet just as fast in downturns. Imagine your portfolio exactly matched the NASDAQ's meteoric rise in a tech boom—exciting, right? Now imagine it also matched the NASDAQ during a tech crash, wiping out a huge chunk of your gains. Suddenly, not keeping up with the index doesn't sound so bad. In fact, it could mean your portfolio is more stable and less vulnerable to the wild swings of the market, especially during turbulent times. So while you might miss out on the extreme highs, you could also protect yourself from the gut-wrenching lows.

Emotional Roller Coaster

Constantly comparing your returns to these skewed benchmarks can trigger emotional decision-making. Remember, emotions can lead you into situations where you're not thinking clearly—much like sneaking out at night to egg houses and setting off firecrackers.

Misaligned Goals

These benchmarks have nothing to do with your personal financial goals. They don't know your name, your retirement dreams, or how many times you've promised your spouse a stress-free vacation. Using them as a measure of success is like trying to fit into someone else's custom-tailored suit.

CRAFTING YOUR PERSONAL BENCHMARK: THE REAL GOLD STANDARD

What's the alternative? Instead of hitching your financial wagon to arbitrary indices, create a benchmark that's as unique as you are.

START WITH A PLAN

Before you even think about which dividend stocks to pick based on everything you're about to learn in this book, you need a plan—a personalized income plan that outlines your financial needs, goals, and timelines. It's not just about picking dividend stocks. It's about understanding how those dividend stocks will fit into your overall financial picture.

We use an income planning software called **Simplicitree**. Yes, we're biased because we created it! The idea behind Simplicitree is to simplify the complex process of income planning, helping you visualize your shortfall (the gap between where you are and where you need to be) and guiding you step-by-step toward creating a sustainable income plan.

If you're not sure where to start, I highly recommend trying it. It's built to help you identify everything I'm going to teach you in the following sections.

Having a solid plan isn't just a "nice to have." It's the foundation of your financial success. A tool like Simplicitree can provide the structure to understand your income needs, project future expenses, and figure out how to bridge the gap. It ensures your investment strategy isn't just a collection of investments—it's a coordinated effort to meet your personal financial goals, protect your future income, and give you the confidence to enjoy your retirement without worrying about whether your next paycheck is coming from the whims of the market.

IDENTIFY YOUR SHORTFALL

Before you can create a successful income strategy, you must first identify your shortfall—the gap between where you are now and where you want to be financially. Think of it as the difference between your current income or savings and the amount of income you'll need to live comfortably for the rest of your life. It's not just a number; it's the core problem you need to solve.

Planning your income strategy without knowing your shortfall is impossible. Imagine trying to build a house without knowing what the structure should look like, or worse, trying to get healthy by taking random pills without knowing what's wrong with you. You wouldn't go to a drugstore and randomly pick a medicine hoping it would help. But that's exactly what many investors do when they plan their financial future without first understanding their income shortfall. They pick random investments, hoping they'll work, but they don't know what problem they're trying to solve.

Knowing your shortfall is like getting a diagnosis before treatment; it gives you clarity on the problem and the goal. Once you know how much income you need to cover your future expenses, you have a destination to aim for. From there, strategizing to solve it becomes much easier. You're no longer blindly selecting investments, hoping they'll generate enough income; instead, you're building an income-focused strategy designed to close your shortfall gap.

What if you set off on a cross-country road trip without any idea how much gas you'll need to get there? You know your car runs on fuel, but you don't know how far you're going or where the next gas station is. Without that basic knowledge, how can you plan your trip? You'll either stall out in the middle of nowhere or you'll overprepare, wasting time and money on things you don't need.

Your financial journey is no different. Identifying your shortfall gives you the destination—the income target you need to reach. Once you know that, you can map out exactly how to get there, choosing investments and strategies that align with your goals. Whether it's dividend-growth stocks, bonds, or other income-generating assets, the strategy becomes clear when you know what you're aiming for. Without that target, you're just hoping you'll land on the right solution, but you'll never be certain if you're on track.

Again, we use Simplicitree to help clients identify their shortfall. The software considers your current income, future needs, expected inflation, and more to calculate the exact gap you need to close. Once you have that number, everything else falls into place. You're no longer planning blindfolded, but with a clear vision and actionable strategy. This is the cornerstone of successful financial planning and the key to building a retirement without stress or uncertainty.

BUILD A CUSTOM STRATEGY

With your goals and shortfall clearly identified, the next step is to craft an investment strategy that's tailored to your specific income needs.

This is where everything you'll learn in this book about dividend-growth investing will come into play.

Dividend-growth investing isn't just about picking stocks that pay dividends—it's about understanding the underlying forces that drive sustainable, growing income. It's about finding companies with strong financial health, consistent dividend growth, and a history of rewarding shareholders, even during tough market conditions.

If you're worried about having a strategy right now, don't be. We will explore every aspect of why dividend-growth investing is such a powerful strategy. We'll discuss everything from the importance of reinvesting dividends for compounding growth to selecting companies with healthy balance sheets and much more. You'll have plenty of info at the ready when it's time to build your personal dividend income strategy—one that will help you meet your shortfall.

If you're like most investors, then your dividend-growth strategy will form the core of your portfolio and provide a steady, reliable stream of income. But it's important to remember you don't have to rely solely on dividend stocks to meet your income needs. Depending on your shortfall and personal circumstances, you might consider adding other income-generating assets to complement your dividend portfolio.

When you combine dividend-growth stocks with other income-generating assets, you create a strategy designed to meet your income needs, both now and in the future. More importantly, it's a strategy that aligns with your personal financial goals—helping you not only solve the shortfall but create a surplus of income that can sustain you throughout retirement.

MEASURE WHAT MATTERS

When it comes to tracking your progress, the standard benchmarks like the S&P 500 and NASDAQ fall short. As we've already discussed, a few dominant companies and sectors skewed these indices, making them poor measures for your personal financial success. So, if you don't use those benchmarks, what do you use?

The answer is simple: Your unique benchmark is your income shortfall, whether your strategy is generating the income you need each year to solve it. The proper measure of success isn't about beating the S&P 500 or matching the NASDAQ. It's about ensuring your investments provide the income you need to live the life you've envisioned for your future.

Here's why this matters: When you figure out what income you'll need in retirement, you're not just guessing at a number. You're setting a target that becomes your personal benchmark. It's unique to you because it's based on your lifestyle, your future expenses, and your goals. That's the only accurate measure of your financial success—not whether you kept up with an arbitrary index, but whether you're on track to generate the income required to live comfortably.

Imagine if your shortfall income goal in retirement is to have $80,000 per year. That's your benchmark. Each year, you need to measure whether your dividend-growth strategy, combined with any other income sources you have, is generating $80,000 (adjusted for inflation and taxes). If so, you are succeeding. If it's not, you need to adjust your strategy—not because you didn't beat the S&P, but because you need to close that gap and cover your shortfall.

It's like training for a marathon. You don't measure your progress by how fast Usain Bolt runs a 100-meter dash—he's not running the same race you are. Instead, you track your pace, stamina, and distance against the goal you've set for yourself. Your success depends on whether you can finish the race you're training for, not how well someone else is running a different one.

By using your income needs as your benchmark, you can filter out the noise of market volatility, headlines about the NASDAQ's performance, or the S&P's latest high. Those metrics simply don't matter when it comes to your financial well-being. What matters is that your portfolio delivers the consistent, reliable income you need to support your future.

This approach doesn't just give you a clearer target—it gives you peace of mind. You're no longer caught up in the stress of chasing market returns. Instead, you focus on what truly matters: solving your shortfall, growing your income, and ensuring your investment strategy aligns with your goals. It's a more personal, purposeful way to measure success and, ultimately, a far more effective way to manage your investments.

So when you sit down to review your progress, don't ask, "Did I beat the market?" Instead, ask, "Am I generating the income I need to live my retirement dream?" That's the only benchmark that matters, and it's one that's built specifically for you.

DON'T RIDE SOMEONE ELSE'S ROLLER COASTER: YOUR MOMENT OF TRUTH

The next time you catch yourself glancing at the S&P 500 or the NASDAQ and feeling a twinge of envy or panic, remember that those indices are on their own journey—a journey that doesn't align with your destination.

On that note, be the architect of your own financial future. Just like the night I faced the consequences of my actions rather than follow Johnny into the woods, you have the power to make decisions that align with your long-term goals. By charting your own course, you're in the driver's seat, steering toward a future tailored to your dreams and needs.

Remember, your financial journey is as individual as your fingerprint. Celebrate that uniqueness by creating a plan and benchmark that reflect your personal goals.

Investing isn't about keeping up with the Joneses, or the Dow

Jones, for that matter. It's about securing your financial future in a way that's aligned with your life, your values, and your aspirations.

Stay focused on what matters:

- **Personal Goals over Public Indices:** Let your financial plan be your guide, not the daily fluctuations of the market.
- **Emotional Discipline:** Keep emotions in check to make rational, informed decisions.
- **Continuous Review:** Regularly assess your progress toward your goals and adjust your strategy as needed.

Embarking on your own path may seem daunting, but remember, every great journey starts with a single step. And unlike that night of mischief, this is one adventure where taking responsibility and forging your own path will lead to rewarding destinations.

In the grand scheme, benchmarks like the S&P 500 and the NASDAQ are just impersonal numbers on a screen. Your personal benchmark, however, reflects your life's ambitions. So why settle for someone else's map when you can draw your own?

Remember, you are the hero of your financial story. It's time to bench the benchmarks and play the game on your terms.

CAN YOU NAVIGATE THE ICEBERGS IN YOUR PORTFOLIO?

Now that you've learned how overconcentration can sink even the most "unsinkable" portfolios, it's time to focus on steering clear of the next set of potential hazards. In the upcoming chapter, "Titanic Portfolios and Unsinkable Strategies," we'll dive into the strategies that help you avoid common investment pitfalls and guide you through turbulent financial waters.

CHAPTER 3

Titanic Portfolios and Unsinkable Strategies

Putting All Your Eggs in One Basket Could Scramble Your Finances

As advisors, we often see disasters coming from a mile away, even when the people involved remain blissfully unaware, convinced that loyalty or familiarity with a company will protect them from financial ruin. I want to share two quick stories from my career that highlight the importance of learning from the mistakes of others and the value of risks that hide in plain sight.

SEEING UNSEEN RISKS

The first happened early in my career. I sat across from a prospective client, a man whose entire financial life was tied to a single company: General Motors. GM was more than just his workplace or an investment; it was part of his family's legacy. His father and grandfather had dedicated their careers to the company. Every paycheck, he funneled a bit more into GM stock. He viewed it as more than a retirement plan; it was a badge of honor, an "invincible" asset that had stood the test of time.

He was interviewing me to see if I could add any value to his situation, though I sensed he wasn't very open to change. As I reviewed his portfolio, alarm bells were ringing. Nearly all his wealth resided in one stock, one company.

I tried to offer a balanced perspective, suggesting diversification to mitigate risk. He was steadfast. "It's GM," he said with unwavering confidence. "It's always good for us."

Fast-forward a year from that meeting, when "invincible GM" declared bankruptcy.[8] The stock plummeted and wiped out massive amounts of wealth in the blink of an eye. Many of those loyal workers who had poured their savings into the company they trusted saw their portfolios reduced to almost nothing.

The second story happened years later, after I'd moved to Charlotte. This time, it involved employees from American Airlines. My clients didn't hold massive amounts of the company's stock, but many of them relied heavily on something just as fragile: their pensions.[9] When American Airlines declared bankruptcy, many employees saw their pensions slashed to pennies on the dollar. Once again, years of loyalty and trust evaporated overnight.

Both stories highlight a crucial lesson: What's obvious to some remains invisible to others. It's like that classic horror movie moment when the leading character says, "Let's split up!" and you're munching popcorn, thinking, "Well, this will not end well."

These stories also highlight the dangers of overconcentration

---

8 *General Motors 2009 Annual Report* (General Motors Company Form 10-K, 2010), https://investor.gm.com/sec-filings/sec-filing/10-k/0001193125-10-078119; Andrew Clark, "General Motors Declares Bankruptcy—The Biggest Manufacturing Collapse in US History," June 1, 2009, https://www.theguardian.com/business/2009/jun/01/general-motors-bankruptcy-chapter-11.

9 PBGC Case Study "American Airlines Pension Plans" 2015.

and the unseen risks that can jeopardize your financial future. The employees trusted in the invincibility of their employers, blind to the vulnerabilities that others could plainly see. They didn't diversify, didn't adjust, and ultimately paid the price. Their stories serve as a reminder that no single company, no matter how solid its reputation, is immune to catastrophe.

Just as excessive faith in a single company blindsided them, many investors similarly fail to maintain balanced, diversified portfolios. The dangers of overconcentration and lack of balance are risks that are obvious to some but hard to see for most.

LEARNING FROM OTHERS TO ACHIEVE BALANCE

In Chapter 2, I discussed how benchmarks like the S&P 500 and NASDAQ might not be the best measures of success because of their concentration in a few large companies. I also mentioned how following these benchmarks could mislead us. Now I want to look at the S&P 500 differently. Reason: We can learn valuable lessons about balance from it.

By understanding how the S&P 500 is structured and how different weighting methods affect its performance, we can gain insights into how to keep our portfolios balanced and avoid repeating others' mistakes.

ALL INDEXES ARE NOT CREATED EQUALLY

Many investors, in the quest for diversification, turn to indices like the S&P 500. It sounds great in theory—five hundred large US companies representing the broad economy. Surely, you're diversified, right?

Well, not quite. Plot twist: The S&P 500 plays favorites like a grandparent with a favorite grandchild. It's a market-cap-weighted index: The bigger the company, the bigger slice of the pie it controls.

Currently, giants like Apple and Microsoft represent over 14 percent of the total index. Just imagine if the fortunes of those companies plummet. Your portfolio could take a massive hit despite being "diversified" across five hundred companies.

This concentration is like the unseen risks that the GM and American Airlines employees faced. Their belief in security stemmed from the company's size and reputation, but they didn't realize their heavy exposure to a single point of failure.

EQUAL WEIGHTING: STRIVING FOR TRUE BALANCE

What if we could ensure each company got an equal share of the investment pie? That's where the S&P 500 Equal Weight Index comes in. Unlike its market-cap-weighted counterpart, this index gives each company the same influence. Apple gets the same weight as a company like Domino's pizza, because in this index, whether you're selling smartphones or stuffed crusts, everyone gets an equal slice.

By equal weighting, we achieve a more balanced portfolio, reducing the risk that performance of a few large companies will heavily affect our investments. This approach helps us see and mitigate risks that might be invisible in a market-cap-weighted index.

Research shows that over time, the equal-weighted version of the S&P 500 has often outperformed the traditional market-cap-weighted index. From 1990 to 2009, the equal-weighted index outperformed by around 1.8 percent annually.[10] Why? Because when smaller or less-known companies start doing well, the equal-weighted index captures their growth more effectively. The market-cap index is all about riding the waves of the big players, which can be a problem if those sectors decide to tank.

Let me illustrate just how significant that seemingly small 1.8

10 S&P DJI paper "S&P 500 Equal Weight Index. Twenty Years of History" 2010 update, Exhibit 3.

percent difference can be. Imagine two investors: Alex and Jordan. In 1990, both invested $100,000—Alex in the traditional market-cap-weighted S&P 500 index, and Jordan in the equal-weighted S&P 500 index. Over the next twenty years, Alex's investment grows at an average annual rate of 8percent, while Jordan's grows at 9.8 percent per year because of the extra 1.8 percent annual return from the equal-weighted index.

By 2009, Alex's investment in the standard S&P 500 would have grown to $466,100, while Jordan's investment would have grown to about $645,700 in the equally weighted S&P 500. That's a difference of about $180,000, a staggering 38 percent more, just from that additional 1.8 percent annual return.

Think about that for a moment. An extra 1.8 percent per year doesn't sound like much on the surface, but over two decades it translates into a substantially larger nest egg. This example demonstrates the power of compound interest and how small advantages can snowball into significant gains over time.

This isn't just about numbers; it's a lesson in the importance of balance and diversification. By equal weighting their investments, investors like Jordan capture growth across a broader spectrum of companies, not just the market giants. This approach can lead to higher returns and reduced risk—key principles we can apply to our portfolios to avoid the pitfalls others have encountered.

The extra 1.8 percent annual return achieved by the equal-weighted index over the market-cap-weighted index is a significant change. It shows that sometimes the best-kept secrets are hidden in plain sight. By learning from this research on balance, we can make more informed decisions that align with our long-term goals.

THE POWER OF REBALANCING: KEEP YOUR PORTFOLIO ALIGNED

Even with the equal-weighted index, some companies will grow faster than others. Left unchecked, that "equal weight" you started with can quickly turn into an uneven stack of holdings. Enter rebalancing, the strategy of selling off a bit of the top performers and redistributing those profits into the laggards to maintain balance.

Think of rebalancing like giving your portfolio a regular oil change. Skip it, and things might start to smoke—and not in a good way. Without regular adjustments, parts can wear differently, leading to breakdowns. Rebalancing keeps your portfolio running smoothly, ensuring no single investment grows disproportionately and introduces hidden risks.

For example, during the 2008 financial crisis, a rebalanced portfolio experienced a smaller drop compared to a portfolio that wasn't rebalanced. By regularly adjusting your holdings, you manage risk and keep your investment strategy aligned with your goals.

DIVIDENDS: THE UNSUNG HERO OF LONG-TERM INVESTING

Let's bring things back to dividends—those powerhouses behind long-term investment growth. While many focus on capital appreciation (the increase in stock prices), the truth is that over time dividends play a massive role in total returns over time.

From 1930 to 2020, dividends accounted for approximately **42 percent** of the S&P 500's total return. But when you reinvest those dividends, their impact becomes even more significant, contributing to **over 60 percent** of the S&P 500's total return during that period.[11]

---

11 Hartford Funds, *The Power of Dividends: Past, Present, and Future* (2025) 2, https://www.hartfordfunds.com/dam/en/docs/pub/whitepapers/WP106.pdf.

To truly grasp the importance of dividends, consider this: As of recent data, about 84 percent of the companies in the S&P 500 pay dividends.[12] This means most companies contribute to this powerful engine of growth, underscoring how integral dividends are to the overall performance of the index.

THE OAK TREE ANALOGY

Think of your investment like planting an acorn. Today it's tiny and unimpressive, but with time and patience, it becomes the mighty oak tree that makes your neighbor's sapling look like a houseplant.

The acorn grows into a sapling, which eventually becomes a sturdy oak tree. This tree represents your initial investment growing. Now, imagine this oak tree starts producing acorns of its own. These are your dividends. If you collect those acorns and plant them, you'll grow more oak trees. Each new tree then produces its own acorns, which you can plant again.

Over the years, what started as a single oak tree becomes an entire forest. This forest didn't appear overnight; it grew gradually because you kept planting those acorns. Similarly, reinvesting dividends allows your investment to grow exponentially over time, turning modest beginnings into substantial wealth.

THE MATHEMATICAL IMPACT OF DIVIDENDS

To highlight how substantial dividends can be, let's look at some numbers. Suppose you invested $10,000 in the S&P 500 at the beginning of 1980. If you relied solely on capital appreciation (price returns) and

---

12 S&P Dow Jones Indices, "Dividend Growth Picks Up Third Quarter," press release, October 7, 2014, https://www.spglobal.com/spdji/en/documents/index-news-and-announcements/20141007-dividends.pdf?utm_source=chatgpt.com.

didn't reinvest dividends, your investment would have grown to about **$760,000** by the end of 2020. Not bad, right?

But if you had reinvested your dividends during that same period, your $10,000 would have grown to approximately **$1.97 million.** That's an increase of over **$1.2 million** thanks to reinvested dividends—a difference of over **160 percent** compared to not reinvesting dividends.

This dramatic difference showcases how reinvested dividends significantly amplify your returns over the long term. It's not just a slight improvement; it's a transformational impact on your wealth accumulation.

DIVIDENDS AS A KEY DRIVER OF GROWTH

Dividends are like the secret ingredient in Grandma's famous cookies—you might not see them, but they're what makes everything taste so amazing. Companies that consistently pay and increase dividends often show strong financial health and a commitment to shareholder value. By focusing on dividend-paying stocks, you're investing in companies with solid fundamentals and sustainable business models. We will go over a lot more about this later.

Reinvesting dividends takes advantage of dollar-cost averaging. When you automatically reinvest dividends, you're purchasing more shares regardless of the stock price, which can lower your average cost per share over time and reduce the impact of market volatility.

CONNECTING THE DOTS: DIVIDENDS AND REBALANCING, A POWERFUL SYNERGY

Knowing that approximately 84 percent of S&P 500 companies pay dividends helps explain why dividends are the bedrock of growth within the index. Dividends aren't just occasional bonuses. They're a significant driver of total returns over time. When reinvested, dividends compound, accelerating your portfolio's growth in a way that's both consistent and powerful.

Here's where the magic truly happens: Combining the steady strength of dividend-paying stocks with the strategic practice of rebalancing can lead to even greater success and returns.

Rebalancing isn't just about maintaining a set allocation; it's about actively managing your investments to capitalize on opportunities and mitigate risks.

HOW DIVIDENDS AND REBALANCING WORK TOGETHER

1. **Dividends Fuel Compounded Growth:** Reinvesting dividends means purchasing more shares of dividend-paying stocks. This increases your dividend income over time with no additional capital investment. It's like planting seeds that grow into trees, which then produce more seeds, leading to a flourishing forest.
2. **Rebalancing Enhances Returns:** As certain stocks outperform others, your portfolio can become unbalanced, overweighted in high-performing stocks and underweighted in others. By rebalancing—selling a portion of the overperforming stocks and buying more of the underperforming but fundamentally strong dividend payers—you lock in gains and position yourself for future growth. This "buy low, sell high" strategy can boost your overall returns.
3. **Risk Management Through Diversification:** Rebalancing ensures you're not excessively exposed to any single company or sector. Just as the employees of GM and American Airlines learned the hard way, overconcentration can be detrimental. By maintaining a diversified portfolio of dividend-paying stocks across various sectors, you mitigate the risk of any single investment harming your wealth.

AN ILLUSTRATION OF THE SYNERGY

Imagine your portfolio is a well-tended garden. Dividends are the perennials that keep blooming, and rebalancing is your trusty pair of gardening shears. Without them, things get wild enough to star in their own jungle adventure.

Meanwhile, rebalancing is the act of pruning and replanting… cutting back the overgrown areas and nurturing the parts that need more attention. Without pruning, some plants might overtake others, leading to an unbalanced garden that doesn't produce well.

By regularly rebalancing, you ensure all parts of your garden contribute to a bountiful harvest.

THE MATHEMATICAL IMPACT

Let's play with some numbers. Suppose you start with a $100,000 investment in a diversified portfolio of dividend-paying stocks within the S&P 500.

Historically, the average annual return of the S&P 500, including dividends, is about **10 percent.**[13] However, by actively rebalancing your portfolio and focusing on dividend reinvestment, you might enhance your returns by an additional **1.8 percent** annually, similar to the outperformance of the equal-weighted index over the market-cap-weighted index.

Over the next twenty years, here's how that plays out:

- Without Rebalancing (10 percent annual return):
    - Future Value = $\$100,000 \times (1 + 0.10)^{20} \approx \$672,750$
- With Rebalancing and Dividend Focus (11.8 percent annual return):
    - Future Value = $\$100,000 \times (1 + 0.118)^{20} \approx \$901,130$

13 J.P. Morgan Asset Management, *Guide to the Markets (Q1 2025)*, January 2025, https://am.jpmorgan.com/us/en/asset-management/adv/insights/market-insights/guide-to-the-markets/.

That's an additional **$228,380** in wealth...over **34 percent** more—thanks to the combined power of dividends and rebalancing.

By combining dividend reinvestment with regular rebalancing, you're not just planting seeds and hoping for rain; you're watering, weeding, and maybe even doing a little growth dance when no one's watching. Dividends create a steady stream of income and growth, and rebalancing optimizes this growth and manages risks.

This strategy helps you:

- **Capture Gains:** Lock in profits from overperforming stocks—kind of like cashing in your chips while you're still on a winning streak in Vegas.
- **Buy Opportunities:** Invest in quality undervalued dividend-paying companies. It's like finding designer clothes at a thrift store.
- **Maintain Balance:** Avoid overexposure to any single stock or sector—because no one wants their portfolio to resemble a one-hit wonder.
- **Enhance Compounding:** Accelerate growth through reinvested dividends and strategic allocation—think of it as your money making money babies.

Moral of the story: Dividends are the foundation—the bedrock—of long-term growth in the S&P 500. They offer a reliable source of returns that, when reinvested, significantly boost your portfolio's value over time. Rebalancing acts as the mechanism that keeps your investment strategy aligned with your goals, ensuring you continue to benefit from the strengths of dividend-paying stocks while minimizing potential risks.

By bringing these two powerful strategies together, you position yourself to achieve greater success and returns. It's not just about recognizing the importance of dividends or the necessity of rebalancing; it's about understanding how they complement each other to create a robust, resilient investment approach.

The combination of dividend investing and regular rebalancing is a lesson in seeing the obvious advantages that are often overlooked. Just as some investors cannot see the risks of overconcentration, others might miss the profound impact of these synergistic strategies.

By connecting the dots between dividends as the foundation for growth and rebalancing as a driver of enhanced returns, you can build an investment strategy that not only avoids common pitfalls but also seizes opportunities for greater financial success.

TIME TO PUT YOUR INVESTMENT PHILOSOPHY INTO ACTION

Before we go forward, let's review some of what we've learned so far:

- Not all indexes are created equal.
- The market-cap-weighted approach can expose you to undue risk from a handful of giant companies, much like the overconcentration seen in the stories earlier.
- Embracing an equal-weighted strategy of dividend stocks can provide true diversification, capturing growth across a broader spectrum of companies and leading to potentially higher returns over time.
- Rebalancing is the tool that keeps your portfolio aligned with your goals, preventing any single investment from dominating your holdings. Coupled with the power of dividends—the bedrock of long-term growth—reinvesting these payouts and regularly adjusting your portfolio can significantly enhance your wealth accumulation.

Ultimately, keeping your portfolio in check means being proactive, vigilant, and willing to adjust your strategy as needed. Balance and diversification aren't just buzzwords; they're essential principles that can protect your wealth and help it grow. By applying these lessons, you're not only avoiding the pitfalls that others have encountered, but also positioning yourself for greater financial success in the future.

As for what's next: We'll dive deeper into how you can craft and implement your own investment philosophy. It's one thing to know you need a plan; it's another to build one that's as sturdy and reliable as a well-built vessel.

CHAPTER 4

Charting Your Course to Financial Independence

How a Seasick Fishing Trip Taught Me the Importance of Planning

LOST AT SEA: MY FIRST FISHING FIASCO

Ever dive headfirst into something new, only to realize you're in over your head? Let me amuse you with the first time I ever went fishing—a humbling experience that taught me more about planning than any business seminar ever could. It's not just a funny story to share over dinner (though it does get a few laughs). It's also a metaphor for investing.

I found myself in Jupiter, Alaska (yes, it's about as remote as it sounds), gearing up for an epic fishing adventure with a group of seasoned anglers. These guys were the real deal. They talked about reels and rods like artists discuss brushes and paints. Me? I was just excited to wear the cool fishing gear I bought online.

We woke up at an hour I never knew existed (I'm pretty sure we woke up the roosters) and headed to the Jupiter marina. The excitement was electric—we were like kids on Christmas morning. The journey to our fishing spot took about two and a half hours. On the way, we blasted music and chowed down on breakfast sandwiches, and the camaraderie was awesome. I couldn't wait to catch my first big fish!

As soon as we reached the spot and the boat stopped, reality hit me—hard. The waves began tossing the boat around like a cork in a washing machine. The nautical roller coaster tossed us up and down, and my stomach was not amused. Before I knew it, I was leaning over the side, contributing my breakfast to the depths below. Let's just say I was "chumming the waters" in the most literal sense.

For the next six hours, I became intimately acquainted with the side of the boat. I didn't touch a fishing pole. Heck, I could hardly stand. All I could think about was how to get off this floating torture chamber. My grand vision of reeling in a trophy fish was replaced by a singular goal: survival.

Meanwhile, the captain and my buddies were unfazed. They had a plan, knew what to expect, and executed flawlessly. They caught fish after fish, laughing and sharing stories, while I contemplated how realistic it could be for me to swim back to shore.

Eventually, mercy came in the form of trolling near the shore. The steady movement eased my seasickness, and miraculously, I caught a fish! It wasn't the monstrous catch I'd imagined, but given the circumstances, it felt like I'd conquered Moby Dick.

Looking back, it's clear I was unprepared. I jumped into something without a plan or an understanding of what to expect. The seasoned fishermen and the captain had experience and a strategy; they knew how to navigate both calm and stormy waters. Me? I was at the mercy of the waves and my naivety.

Jumping into financial markets without a solid investment philosophy can be pretty similar to hopping on a boat without sea legs or a clue. You're likely to end up feeling sick, disoriented, and desperate to get out.

WHAT ON EARTH IS AN INVESTMENT PHILOSOPHY?

Think of an investment philosophy as your financial GPS—a set of guiding principles that inform every decision you make with your money. More than a strategy, it's your investment DNA, unique to you but grounded in proven principles that pave the way for long-term success.

Without an investment philosophy, you're vulnerable to every wave and current that comes your way. On my fishing trip, my lack of preparation had me tossed around like my dignity stuck in the spin cycle. Similarly, investors without a guiding philosophy are at the mercy of market volatility, reacting impulsively rather than navigating thoughtfully.

Once I adopted a simple plan—like focusing on trolling near the shore where the waters were calmer—I enjoyed the experience and even caught a fish. In investing, having a well-defined philosophy allows you to stay the course, make informed decisions, and ultimately achieve your financial goals.

YOUR SECRET SAUCE

You should have a singular, straightforward mission: to achieve financial independence through dividend investing. You should not be about chasing the latest fads or trying to time the market. (Spoiler alert: No one has a functioning crystal ball.) Instead, focus on what you can control: generating steady, predictable income.

RELIABLE INCOME

In a world where stock prices can fluctuate faster than my stomach on that fishing boat, dividends are the dependable friend who always shows up. Dividend-paying companies share a portion of their profits with you, rain or shine. If you are someone nearing or enjoying retirement, this predictable income can be the bedrock of your financial security. It's like having a boat that doesn't make you seasick, no matter how rough the waters get.

But it's not just about the income. The beauty of dividend-paying stocks is their potential for long-term growth. As these companies expand, so do their dividends. It's the financial equivalent of finally catching that fish after hours of struggle—a reward that makes the journey worthwhile.

WHY DIVIDENDS ARE THE BEE'S KNEES

Think of dividend stocks like your go-to life vest: reliable, comforting, and always there to keep you afloat. Even when the market's waters get choppy, dividends keep rolling in. You might feel uneasy watching those sudden swells, but it's reassuring to know your dividend "lifeline" arrives right on schedule, market tantrums and all. That steady buoyancy is priceless, especially when you're charting your course for retirement.

One of the biggest worries investors share is, "Will I have enough income to live the retirement I want?" Dividend investing can help calm those fears. By aiming for a solid dividend yield—say, around 6 percent—you can generate the income you need to navigate life's journey without constantly fretting over the storms in your portfolio. It's like having a dependable anchor, minus the risk of it failing when you need stability most.

Dividends don't just provide immediate income; they can also grow over time. As companies increase their payouts, your income rises, helping you stay ahead of inflation's tide. If you're worried about rising costs eating into your retirement savings, focusing on dividend growth stocks can ensure your income stays on course. While others might be bailing water over rising coffee prices, you'll be more focused on planning your next big voyage.

THE PILLARS HOLDING UP YOUR FINANCIAL TEMPLE

Successful investing is like regular boat maintenance—consistency is key, even when you're tempted to skip crucial checks. Markets will roll like rough seas, but sticking to your navigation plan keeps you from making rash moves. Take my client Linda, for example, who's feeling something we can all relate to. When the market took a dive, she felt like bailing on everything—ready to jump ship and hoard emergency provisions. But she circled back to her long-term strategy, focused on dividend growth, and held firm. A few months later, her portfolio was not just afloat; it was sailing smoothly.

Being a discerning investor is crucial—think of it like a seasoned angler who only trusts well-maintained gear and proven fishing spots. It's vital to focus on companies with solid financials, a history of rising dividends, and strong growth potential. Don't be dazzled by flashy newcomers that promise the moon but might sink at the first sign of big waves.

Remember: It's not about snagging quick catches that flop off the hook the moment you reel them in. The goal is to invest in stable, seaworthy companies with strong "hulls" and proven track records. It's like choosing a dependable trawler over a flashy speedboat that might break down after just a few trips. When you prioritize durability and reliability, you're setting sail toward a more secure financial future.

THE BIG CATCH: STOCK GROWTH FROM AN INVESTOR'S PERSPECTIVE

Here's the delightful twist: When you invest in robust, dividend-paying companies, stock growth often follows. Not only do you enjoy consistent income from dividends, but over the years, the value of your stocks can increase significantly. It's like buying a house and discovering oil in the backyard.

Dividend growth and stock appreciation are the dynamic duo of investing. As companies prosper, they increase their dividend payouts, and their stock prices often rise. It benefits everyone involved—a bit like finding out your favorite pizza place also gives you free dessert with every order.

By focusing on companies with solid financials and a history of increasing dividends, you set yourself up for both immediate income and long-term growth. It's not just about the dividends or the stock appreciation alone; it's about how they work together to boost your overall returns. Investing this way can feel like you've hit the jackpot twice—with the same ticket.

YOUR PROVEN RECIPE FOR SUCCESS

You don't throw darts at a list of stocks (though that might make for an entertaining evening). Instead, your approach to discovering, tracking, and managing dividend portfolios is methodical and proven. You delve into financial statements, assess market conditions, and evaluate company leadership. There's a little detective work in this (with fewer trench coats but more spreadsheets).

Markets can be unpredictable and sometimes downright unpleasant. That's why you continually monitor and adjust your portfolio to align with changing market conditions and your evolving needs. You're proactive, not reactive, ensuring your investments are always positioned for success.

WHY YOU NEED YOUR OWN FINANCIAL NORTH STAR

The market is a noisy place filled with "can't miss" opportunities and doom-and-gloom predictions. Without a solid investment philosophy, it's easy to get swept up in the latest craze. Perhaps you've seen others jump on the cryptocurrency bandwagon without understanding it, only to be left holding digital coins worth less than arcade tokens. Avoiding the herd isn't just wise—it's profitable.

Having an investment philosophy brings consistency and peace of mind. Well-thought-out principles root your decisions, so you don't let every market fluctuation sway you. It's like having an umbrella in a rainstorm—you might not control the weather, but you're prepared for it.

By establishing your own guiding principles, you equip yourself to make informed decisions rather than reactive ones. This approach helps you stay focused on your long-term goals, even when the market tries to distract you with its highs and lows. In the end, a well-defined investment philosophy isn't just a strategy—it's your financial compass, steering you toward lasting success.

KNOWLEDGE: THE BEST INVESTMENT YOU CAN MAKE

You believe that being informed makes you a more confident investor. You don't just hand over your money and hope for the best; you strive to understand the "why" behind your investment strategies. When you grasp the reasoning, you're less likely to make fear-based decisions during market downturns. It's the difference between being a passenger and a copilot on your financial journey.

Education fosters confidence, and confidence leads to better investment outcomes. By demystifying the process, you equip yourself to stay the course, even when the financial seas get choppy. After all, you can weather the storm more easily when you know your ship is built to last.

PUTTING IT ALL TOGETHER

We've journeyed through the highs and lows of investing, much like my first (and somewhat disastrous) fishing trip. We've talked about the importance of having a solid plan, staying disciplined, and focusing on quality. Now, it's time to pull back the curtain.

Let me share with you the investment philosophy that guides the financial decisions we make at Insight Folios, my RIA. This same compass might help you chart your own course toward financial independence.

WHY WE CHOOSE DIVIDEND INVESTING

At Insight Folios, we are driven by a single, unwavering mission: to empower our clients to achieve financial independence and peace of mind through the power of dividend investing.

In a world of market unpredictability and economic uncertainties, we believe in the stability and reliability of quality dividend stocks. These stocks not only provide a steady income but also offer the potential for growth, making them a cornerstone of a resilient retirement portfolio.

Predictable Income

In the ever-fluctuating landscape of stock markets, predicting growth can be akin to chasing the wind. However, dividend income stands as a beacon of stability. It offers a more predictable and consistent return, which is vital for our clients, many of whom are seeking to bridge the gap in their retirement income.

Retirement Income Solutions

A significant number of our clients face a daunting challenge: a shortfall in their retirement income. We tailor our approach to address this issue head-on by generating consistent dividend income. We target a robust 6 percent dividend yield, providing our clients with the reliable income they need to maintain and enhance their lifestyle in retirement.

Quality and Growth

Our commitment extends beyond just current dividend income. We seek sustainable income that is positioned for growth. By focusing on stocks with a history of dividend increases, we aim to shield our clients from the eroding effects of inflation, thereby preserving and enhancing their purchasing power over time.

Stock Growth

While our primary focus is on dividend income, we also believe that sound financials lead to strong stock growth. When a company shows robust financial health and a reliable history of dividend payouts, stock growth is a natural by-product. By identifying companies with strong financials and a proven dividend track record, we aim to secure not only steady income but also significant capital appreciation for clients of any age.

PROVEN STRATEGY

Our team at Insight Folios has developed a proven strategy to discover, track, change, and manage dividend portfolios. We meticulously research and select stocks that not only offer attractive yields but also exhibit strong potential for continued growth and reliability. This disciplined approach positions our clients to potentially benefit from the best opportunities the market has to offer.

OUR COMMITMENT

Our commitment to our clients is unwavering. We strive to build and manage portfolios that deliver both immediate income and long-term growth. Our investment philosophy goes beyond mere financial returns; it is about providing peace of mind and securing financial futures.

By focusing on dividend investing, we aim to offer our clients a steady and growing income stream, helping them achieve their retirement goals with confidence and ease. We are dedicated to ensuring that our clients experience the true value of their investments, knowing that their financial well-being is in capable and caring hands.

REELING IT ALL IN

A well-defined investment philosophy is your financial compass, guiding you through the market's ups and downs. It keeps you grounded, focused, and disciplined, leading to consistent, long-term success. Without it, you're just tossing darts in the dark and hoping to hit the bull's-eye.

If you haven't established your own investment philosophy, there's no time like the present. And if you have one, consider revisiting it to ensure it still aligns with your goals. The stronger your guiding principles, the smoother your financial journey will be.

As the legendary Warren Buffett once quipped, "The stock market is a device for transferring money from the impatient to the patient." So be patient, stay disciplined, and let your investment philosophy be the steady hand that guides you toward financial success.

Speaking of patience, it's one of the three true bedrocks of wealth building. The other two are discipline and smart-investing strategies. We'll dive into each one across the next few chapters, explore other foundations of wealth, and spotlight some of the most important principles that continue to stand the test of time in investing.

CHAPTER 5

The Foundations of Wealth

How Not to Lose Your Shirt in the Stock Market While Keeping Your Sanity Intact

You know that feeling when you walk into a grocery store for "just one thing" and walk out with a cart full of stuff you didn't know you needed? Suddenly, you're the proud owner of exotic cheeses, a pineapple corer, and enough toilet paper to survive the next apocalypse. Investing can be a bit like that. Without a plan, you might end up with a portfolio that's a hot mess of random stocks—or worse, a financial future that's as unpredictable as your next impulse buy.

What if I told you there's a way to shop the investment aisles with a list, a purpose, and maybe even some fun along the way? Welcome to the world where market history and human behavior intersect—a place where understanding the past and knowing yourself can turn you into a savvy investor rather than a cautionary tale told at dinner parties.

A HISTORICAL ROLLER COASTER: STRAP IN OR GET OUT?

Let's take a trip down memory lane—not the kind that involves awkward high school photos, but one that traverses the wild and wooly world of financial markets. Picture the stock market as the world's craziest amusement park ride. Sometimes it's the smooth glide of a merry-go-round; other times, it's a roller coaster that makes you question your life choices.

THE DOT-COM BUBBLE: WHEN PETS.COM WALKED SO CHEWY COULD RUN

Cast your mind back to the late 1990s. People were trading stocks like Pokémon cards, except instead of Charizard, everyone wanted a piece of any company that ended with ".com." You had businesses selling pet supplies online (looking at you, Pets.com) valued higher than companies that actually made money. It was like everyone collectively decided that profits were so last century.

Then came the crash. Turns out, when a company doesn't have a viable business model, it doesn't matter how snazzy their website is. Investors who'd been dreaming of yachts and private islands were suddenly hoping they could at least afford ramen noodles.

Here's the kicker: Those who had invested in solid companies with a history of paying and increasing dividends were like the folks who brought an umbrella to a surprise rainstorm—not entirely dry, but definitely better off than the guy in the white T-shirt.

THE 2008 FINANCIAL CRISIS: THE HOUSING MARKET'S UNINVITED GUEST

Fast-forward to 2008. Remember when everyone thought housing prices could only go up? Buying a house was like buying a lottery ticket that always paid out. Banks were handing out mortgages like free samples at Costco. "No income? No problem!"

Spoiler alert: This did not end well. When the housing bubble burst, it was like musical chairs where someone removed all the chairs at once. Panic ensued. Markets tanked. But yet again, dividend investors who held onto companies with strong balance sheets found that while their portfolios took a hit, they were still receiving dividend checks. It's like being on a sinking ship but having a life vest—you're wet, but at least you're afloat.

THE COVID-19 CRASH: WHEN TOILET PAPER BECAME MORE VALUABLE THAN OIL

And who could forget March 2020? The world shut down, and suddenly toilet paper became the hottest commodity. The stock market experienced its fastest fall in history, leaving investors feeling like they'd just gone bungee jumping without a cord.

Here's something interesting: Many dividend-paying companies continued to distribute cash to shareholders. Many of these companies even increased their dividends. It was as if these companies said, "Global pandemic? Hold my coffee." They had the free cash flow to support their payouts, demonstrating resilience in the face of unprecedented challenges.

YOUR BRAIN: A GREAT FRIEND AND A TERRIBLE INVESTOR

Now, let's talk about the squishy thing between your ears. It's fantastic for many things: writing poetry, solving crossword puzzles, remembering the lyrics to that song you hate but can't stop singing. But for investing, your brain can be like that friend who always gives the worst advice with the best intentions.

FEAR AND GREED: THE TERRIBLE TWINS

Meet Fear and Greed, the emotional equivalents of eating an entire tub of ice cream at midnight. Fear tells you to sell everything when the market dips—because obviously, the world is ending. Greed whispers that you should put all your money into that "hot new stock" your barber mentioned because it's "going to the moon!"

These emotions can lead to some pretty regrettable decisions, like panic selling at market bottoms or buying into bubbles right before they burst. It's like running out of a haunted house straight into a snake pit.

THE FOMO EFFECT: KEEPING UP WITH THE JONESES, MARKET EDITION

Ever heard your neighbor brag about doubling their money on a "sure thing"? Suddenly, your steady gains feel about as exciting as watching paint dry. That's the Fear of Missing Out (FOMO), and it's as contagious as yawning.

Here's the thing: By the time you hear about these "can't miss" opportunities, others have already made the real profits. Chasing them is like trying to catch the last train after it's already left the station—you just end up looking silly and out of breath.

THE POWER OF NOT DOING ANYTHING (SERIOUSLY)

Imagine planting a tree. You don't dig it up every week to see if the roots are growing, right? Investing, especially in dividend-paying stocks, is a lot like that. It's about patience and letting time do the heavy lifting.

THE MAGIC OF COMPOUNDING: INTEREST'S COOL OLDER SIBLING

I believe it was Albert Einstein who called compound interest the "eighth wonder of the world." I can't confirm he actually said that, but it's a great line, so let's roll with it.

Compounding is earning interest on your interest, dividends on your dividends. It's like a snowball rolling down a hill, gathering more snow (or in this case, money) as it goes. The longer it rolls, the bigger it gets.

For example, if you invested $10,000 in a dividend stock yielding 4 percent and reinvested those dividends, in thirty years, you'd have over $32,000—not because you added more money, but because the dividends you earned bought more shares, which earned more dividends, and so on. It's the financial version of "The Gift That Keeps On Giving." This example doesn't include any market growth; that is growth from the dividend. More on this later.

DIVIDEND REINVESTMENT PLANS (DRIPS): THE LAZY INVESTOR'S DREAM

If you're thinking, "I don't want to deal with manually reinvesting dividends," I've got good news. Dividend reinvestment plans, or DRIPs, automatically use your dividends to buy more shares. It's like setting up a coffee maker to brew before you wake up—minimal effort, maximum satisfaction.

DRIPs take advantage of dollar-cost averaging, buying more shares when prices are low and fewer when they're high. Over time, this can reduce your average cost per share, boosting your returns. Plus, you don't have to do anything. It's investing on autopilot.

FREE CASH FLOW: COMPANIES THAT CAN AFFORD TO PAY YOU

Let me introduce you to my good friend, free cash flow (FCF). Think of FCF as a company's allowance after it pays all its bills. It's the money they can use to pay dividends, buy back stock, or stuff under the corporate mattress. We are going to discuss FCF in a lot more detail in Chapter 10, but for now, let me give you a sneak peek.

WHY FCF MATTERS MORE THAN EARNINGS

In short, earnings can be manipulated. Companies might employ "creative accounting" to make things look rosier than they are. But cash doesn't lie. If a company consistently generates strong free cash flow, it's more likely to sustain and grow its dividends.

Think of earnings as the friend who always talks about how much they're working out, but free cash flow is the friend who actually shows up at the gym.

THE DANGER OF DIVIDEND TRAPS

Not all dividends are created equal. Some companies offer sky-high dividend yields that seem too good to be true—and often are. They might pay out more than they earn, dipping into reserves, or worse, taking on debt to maintain dividends.

It's like a restaurant offering a thirty-two-ounce steak for five dollars. Sure, it's a great deal, but you have to wonder what's wrong with the meat.

THE PSYCHOLOGICAL SAFETY NET OF DIVIDENDS

Receiving regular dividends can help mitigate the anxiety of market fluctuations. It's like getting a paycheck regardless of whether your company's stock price is up or down.

THE EMOTIONAL BENEFIT OF GETTING PAID

When the market takes a nosedive, seeing that dividend hit your account can be a comforting reminder that not all is lost. It's tangible proof that your investments are still working for you.

It's akin to owning a rental property. Even if property values dip, you're still collecting rent. That steady income makes it easier to weather the storm and avoid panic selling.

LESSONS FROM LEGENDARY INVESTORS: THEY KNEW WHAT WAS UP

Let's sprinkle in some wisdom from the greats. I'll start with Warren Buffett, a.k.a. "the Oracle of Omaha." Buffett once said, "Our favorite holding period is forever." He invests in companies with solid fundamentals and holds onto them forever. Many of these companies pay dividends. He's the essence of the tortoise: slow, steady, and wildly successful.

Buffett didn't amass his wealth through risky bets or by chasing the latest market fads. He did it through patience, discipline, and a focus on companies that offer value—including those that pay dividends. If patience is good enough for the Oracle of Omaha, it's probably good enough for us mere mortals.

Then there's Peter Lynch, who emphasized investing in what you understand. Translation: If you can't explain in simple terms how a company makes money, maybe think twice about investing in it. Established businesses with straightforward models—utilities, consumer goods, and healthcare—often pay dividends.

MARKET PREDICTIONS: A FOOL'S ERRAND

Trying to time the market is like trying to predict the weather a month from now. Sure, you might get lucky, but more often than not, you'll end up soaked without an umbrella.

THE FOLLY OF FORECASTING

Economists have predicted nine out of the last five recessions, as the joke goes. The point is, even the experts get it wrong. Rather than anticipating every market move, focus on what you can control: your behavior.

STAYING THE COURSE

Investing is a marathon, not a sprint. Markets will go up, they'll go down, and sometimes they'll do both before lunch. By maintaining a long-term perspective, you're less likely to make knee-jerk reactions that can derail your financial goals.

BUILDING WEALTH: IT'S PERSONAL

Wealth means different things to different people. For some, it's security; for others, it's freedom or the ability to help others.

DEFINE YOUR "WHY"

Understanding your motivations can guide your investment strategy. If your goal is financial independence, dividend investing can provide a stream of income that eventually covers your expenses.

It's like planting an orchard. At first, you're nurturing saplings. Over time, they grow, and eventually, they bear fruit season after season. Before you know it, you're sipping lemonade in the shade of your financial orchard.

AVOID LIFESTYLE INFLATION

As your dividends grow, it's tempting to upgrade your lifestyle—nicer car, bigger house, fancier vacations. But remember, increasing expenses can erode the wealth you're building. It's like filling a bucket with water while drilling holes in the bottom—not exactly efficient.

BE THE TORTOISE, NOT THE HARE

If there's one thing I hope you glean from this chapter, it's that slow and steady often wins the race in investing. By understanding market history and recognizing the psychological pitfalls that trip up so many investors, you're already ahead of the game.

Dividend-growth investing isn't about flashy wins or overnight success. It's about making informed decisions, exercising patience, and letting time and compounding do the heavy lifting.

Next time someone tries to lure you into the latest investment fad, just remember the wisdom of the tortoise. Keep moving forward, stay focused on your goals, and enjoy the journey—even if it means passing up on a get-rich-quick scheme involving alpaca farming that might seem oddly tempting. Remember your grocery store lesson: Avoid tossing random "impulse buys" into your cart, and stick to the essential staples that truly nourish your financial plan.

On that note, let's dive even deeper into the patience-and-focus game of dividends, and see how *waiting* can mean *winning* for building wealth.

CHAPTER 6

The Power of Dividends and Patience

How to Grow Money Trees Without Getting Soil Under Your Nails

You know that sweet moment when you find a forgotten $20 bill in the pocket of your favorite jeans? Suddenly, your day goes from meh to magnificent. It's like Mother Nature decided to buy you a sunny lunch.

Now, imagine that feeling happening over and over again, not because you're perpetually forgetful with cash, but because you've set up a system that keeps rewarding you. Welcome to the magical world of dividends—a place where your money doesn't just sit around lazily but gets up, does a bunch of work, and makes more money.

In this chapter, we're diving deep into the river of cash flow and exploring why patience isn't just a virtue—it's actually the secret ingredient in Grandma's famous wealth-building recipe.

THE CASH FLOW CONUNDRUM: SHOW ME THE MONEY!

Let's kick things off with a tale as old as time—or at least as old as Uncle Larry's get-rich-quick schemes. (And if you don't have your own Uncle Larry, I bet you know someone who does.)

To start, imagine owning a chicken that lays golden eggs daily. Would you sell the chicken for a onetime profit, or would you keep feeding it, enjoying a continuous supply of golden eggs? Dividend-paying stocks are your golden-egg-laying chickens. They provide predictable income, which can be especially comforting when the stock market decides to take a nosedive.

THE TALE OF TWO FRIENDS: SPENDTHRIFT SAM AND CASH FLOW CARL

Okay, let's set the eggs aside and focus on two old friends: Spendthrift Sam and Cash Flow Carl.

Sam was the life of the party. He earned a decent salary and believed that money was meant to be enjoyed *now*. Newest smartphone? Had to have it. Limited-edition sneakers? Bought two pairs. He was the embodiment of the phrase "You can't take it with you."

Carl, on the other hand, was a bit more...let's say, forward-thinking. Instead of splurging on the latest gadgets, he invested in dividend-paying stocks. Every month, he watched his cash flow increase—not because he worked extra hours, but because his money worked for him.

Fast-forward a decade. Sam is still standing in line for the next big thing, wondering why he never seems to get ahead financially. Carl? He's sipping piña coladas on a beach, his expenses covered by the dividends rolling into his account. The moral of the story? Carl tapped into the power of predictable income. You see, cash flow isn't just about having money—it's about creating a self-sustaining income stream that doesn't require you to trade hours for dollars.

PATIENCE: THE NOT-SO-SECRET SAUCE OF SUCCESS

Okay, now let's bring things back to patience, one bedrock I wrote about in Chapter 5. Yes, patience is the elusive quality that's easier to preach than to practice. But when it comes to investing, patience isn't just a nice-to-have; it's the entire game.

THE GREAT BAMBOO STORY

Have you ever heard of Chinese bamboo trees? No? Well, sit tight. When you plant a Chinese bamboo seed, nothing happens for the first year. Or the second. Or the third. Or the fourth. You're watering it, fertilizing it, giving it pep talks, and still—nothing. Then, in the fifth year, something incredible happens. The tree sprouts and grows up to ninety feet in just six weeks!

Was the tree dormant for four years only to grow so fast in the fifth? Or was it developing an extensive root system, laying the groundwork for its monumental growth?

Investing in dividends is a lot like nurturing that bamboo tree. At first, it might feel like watching eggshell-colored paint dry. Your investments aren't skyrocketing overnight. But beneath the surface, your dividends are being reinvested, your shares are accumulating, and one day you wake up to find your portfolio has skyrocketed.

REINVESTING DIVIDENDS: THE SNOWBALL EFFECT OF APPLE TREES

Let's talk about one of the most powerful forces in the universe—not gravity, not love, but compounding. In short, reinvesting your dividends to create a snowball effect that can turn into an avalanche (the good kind).

When I was a kid, my family friends had an apple tree. Every year, it produced more apples than they could ever eat. So what did they do? They didn't let them rot or give them all away. They used some seeds to plant more apple trees.

Over time, one apple tree eventually became an entire orchard. By the time I was old enough to appreciate it, that orchard was producing enough fruit to feed her entire neighborhood—and then some.

Reinvesting dividends works the same way. Instead of taking your dividend payouts and spending them on short-term pleasures (as delightful as they may be), you reinvest them to buy more shares. Those new shares generate their own dividends, which buy even more shares, and so on. It's the financial equivalent of turning one apple tree into an orchard.

WEATHERING THE STORM: DIVIDENDS AS A FINANCIAL UMBRELLA

Like my wife often tells me, life isn't always sunshine and rainbows. The market has its ups and downs, much like a roller coaster designed by a caffeine-fueled engineer. But dividends can serve as your financial umbrella during these inevitable storms.

YIELD ON COST: YOUR PERSONAL FINANCIAL TIME MACHINE

Let's dive into a concept known as "yield on cost." It sounds fancy, but it's straightforward—and incredibly satisfying. To help demonstrate the point, I'll use a coffee shop illustration.

Imagine you buy a cup of coffee today for three dollars. Now, suppose you could lock in that price for life, regardless of how much coffee prices rise in the future. Ten years from now, when everyone's paying six dollars for the same cup, you're still paying three dollars. Feels good, right?

Yield on cost works similarly. If you buy a stock at one hundred dollars with an annual dividend of four dollars, your yield is 4 percent. If over the years the company increases its dividend to eight dollars per share, the yield on *your original cost* is now 8 percent. Meanwhile, new investors buying the stock at $200 get a 4 percent yield.

You're essentially getting a better return because you got in early and held on. It's like being part of an exclusive club where the food and drinks get cheaper the longer you stay.

THE JOY OF GROWING DIVIDENDS

Companies that consistently increase their dividends are like the gift that keeps on giving. Each dividend hike boosts your yield on cost, enhancing your income with no additional investment on your part. It's the closest thing to a financial perpetual motion machine.

For investors, dividends don't just provide financial benefits; they offer emotional ones too. Knowing that you're still receiving income can reduce the stress and anxiety that come with market volatility. It's easier to stick to your long-term plan when you have tangible proof your investments are working for you, even when prices are down and your portfolio is suffering.

DIVIDENDS IN RETIREMENT: THE GOLDEN YEARS LOOK BETTER IN GREEN

Retirement should be a time to enjoy the fruits of your labor, not to worry about whether the market's up or down. Dividends can play a crucial role in making your golden years truly golden.

The Retirement Income Dilemma

Many retirees rely on withdrawing from their principal to cover living expenses, which can be risky. If the market takes a downturn, they may have to sell assets at a loss, depleting their nest egg faster than expected.

Enter dividends. With a well-constructed dividend portfolio, you can generate a steady income stream without touching your principal. It's like living off the interest without dipping into your savings account—a financially sustainable way to enjoy retirement.

PEACE OF MIND IS PRICELESS

Knowing that reliable dividend income covers your expenses can provide immense psychological comfort. You can focus on perfecting your golf swing, traveling the world, or finally writing that novel, rather than stressing over market fluctuations.

DISCIPLINE ISN'T JUST FOR MONKS

Let's face it—sticking to a plan isn't always easy. Temptations abound, from the latest tech IPO to that hot stock tip from your neighbor who "knows a guy." But discipline is the bridge between goals and accomplishment.

THE SIREN SONG OF SPECULATION

In Homer's *Odyssey,* the enchanting songs of the Sirens lure sailors to their doom. In the investing world, these siren songs take the form of speculative investments promising massive returns overnight. Spoiler alert: They often end in financial shipwrecks.

By committing to dividend investing, you're effectively tying yourself to the mast, avoiding the temptation to veer off course. It's not as dramatic as battling mythical creatures, but your future self will thank you.

THE REWARD OF CONSISTENCY

Consider the story of the tortoise and the hare. The hare, confident in his speed, takes a nap mid-race, while the tortoise plods along consistently. We all know how that story ends.

Dividend investing is your tortoise strategy. It may not be flashy or fast, but over time, consistency outperforms sporadic bursts of activity. The race to financial independence is a marathon, not a sprint.

Want some proof? Value investing, which is dividend-paying stocks, has outperformed growth investing by over 4 percent per year—since the beginning of the 1900s. To be clear, that is 4 percent more return each year. Fama-French research, which is cited in discussions of the value-versus-growth debate, supports this data. Despite periods where growth has outperformed, which often happens, value stocks have shown long-term resilience, delivering significant returns over extended periods.

THE BEHAVIORAL EDGE: MASTERING YOUR MONEY MINDSET

Understanding the psychology behind investing can give you a significant advantage. After all, the biggest obstacle to financial success often isn't the market—it's ourselves.

THE MARSHMALLOW EXPERIMENT REVISITED

In the famous Stanford marshmallow experiment, children were offered a choice: one marshmallow now or two if they waited fifteen minutes. The kids who waited generally fared better in life, demonstrating the power of delayed gratification.

Investing requires a similar mindset. Choosing to reinvest dividends rather than spending them now can lead to substantially greater rewards down the line. It's like opting for the two marshmallows—but instead of sugary treats, you're getting financial security.

EMOTIONAL INTELLIGENCE IN INVESTING

Managing emotions is crucial. Fear and greed can lead to impulsive decisions: selling in a panic or buying into bubbles. By focusing on dividend cash flow, you can maintain a level-headed approach and make decisions based on strategy rather than emotion.

So, what have we learned on this wild ride through cash flow and behavioral discipline?

- **Cash Flow Is King:** Dividends provide a steady income stream that can buffer against market volatility and support you in retirement.
- **Patience Pays Off:** Wealth building is a long game. Reinvesting dividends and allowing them to compound can lead to exponential growth.

- **Behavioral Discipline Is Your Secret Weapon:** Mastering your emotions and sticking to your plan is essential for long-term success.
- **Yield on Cost Is a Game Changer:** Investing early in dividends, growers can significantly boost their returns over time.
- **Dividends Provide Peace of Mind:** The psychological benefits of predictable income can't be overstated.

Now I'd like to end with a story. A young man asked a wise old farmer the secret to his bountiful tomato harvests. The farmer smiled and said, "I plant the seeds, water them, and then I wait. I don't dig them up to see if they're growing. I don't abandon them for the next big thing. I tend to them patiently, and they reward me."

The young man, seeking quicker results, ignored this advice. He experimented with different seeds, neglected his plants when they didn't sprout immediately, and chased after the latest farming fads. Come harvest time, his baskets were empty.

Be the wise farmer. Plant your seeds in dividend-paying stocks, tend to them with regular investments and reinvestments, and have the patience to let them grow. In time, you'll reap a harvest that can sustain you for years to come.

Now that we've discussed the art of patience and the power of dividends, let's head into one of the most critical aspects of long-term investing: risk management and emotional stability. In the next chapter, we'll tackle the often-overlooked psychological side of investing, where fear and greed can sabotage even the best-laid financial plans.

CHAPTER 7

Risk Management and Emotional Stability

How to Keep Your Cool When the Market Is Acting like a Toddler in a Toy Store

You know that moment when you're peacefully sipping your morning coffee, and suddenly your phone buzzes with a news alert: "Market Plunges Amid Global Uncertainty!" Your heart skips a beat, your palms get sweaty, and you consider stuffing your cash under the mattress alongside that questionable sweater Aunt Gertrude knitted for you.

Welcome to the roller coaster of investing—a ride filled with exhilarating highs, stomach-churning lows, and the occasional urge to scream into the void. What if I told you there's a way to enjoy the ride with no need of a barf bag? A method to manage risk and maintain emotional stability, even when the market throws a tantrum?

In this chapter, we'll explore how dividend-growth investing can be your financial seat belt, airbag, and calming cup of chamomile tea all rolled into one. We'll dig into the psychology behind market volatility and share some stories (both cautionary and inspiring) to help you master your emotions and keep your investment strategy on track.

THE MARKET'S HAUNTED HOUSE: FEAR, THRILLS, AND SPOOKY SURPRISES

First things first: Let's acknowledge that the stock market can be as unpredictable as a cat on catnip. One day, it's purring with contentment; the next, it's climbing the curtains.

Let's rewind to October 19, 1987—better known as Black Monday. The stock market walked off a cliff, dropping over 22 percent in a single day.[14] Investors were panicking like teenagers in a horror movie, running in every direction with no clear plan.

Amid the chaos, some investors remained unshaken. How? They focused on companies with strong fundamentals and reliable dividends. While others were busy hyperventilating, these steady hands saw an opportunity to buy quality stocks at bargain prices. Their secret weapon? Emotional stability and a focus on long-term rather than short-term values are important.

VOLATILITY: THE MARKET'S MOOD SWINGS AND HOW TO HANDLE THEM

Market volatility is like that unpredictable friend who's either the life of the party or a total buzzkill—no middle ground. But just because the market wakes up on the wrong side of the bed doesn't mean you have to as well.

I once met with two very different clients, both of whom taught

---

14 Donald Bernhart and Marshall Eckblad, "Stock Market Crash of 1987," Federal Reserve History, November 22, 2013, https://www.federalreservehistory.org/essays/stock-market-crash-of-1987.

me a lot about the power of mindset in investing. Let's start with the first.

In the early years of my career, when I was at a large brokerage firm, I sat down with Mark, one of my more anxious clients. Mark was the guy who had his eye on the market 24/7. If a stock dropped half a percent, he was on the phone with me, asking if it was time to sell. He'd read every doom-and-gloom headline, and by the time he got to me, he was in full-on panic mode. Every dip in the market sent him scrambling to unload his stocks, convinced the sky was falling. What is the problem? He usually sold right when things were at their worst—locking in losses that could have easily rebounded if he'd just held tight.

Then there was Sarah, who had a very different approach. She knew the market had its ups and downs, and instead of panicking when stocks fell, she'd take a step back and evaluate the bigger picture. She had a portfolio filled with solid dividend-paying stocks alongside other positions and understood that volatility was just part of the ride. When the market dipped, she didn't rush to sell—she held steady, reinvested her dividends, and sometimes even bought more shares at what she called discounted prices. She was in it for the long haul, and she trusted the strategy she'd set in place.

Fast-forward a few years, and the outcomes are as you'd expect. Mark, despite his best intentions, found himself behind. He was constantly trying to time the market, selling low and missing out on the rebounds. His portfolio suffered not from market volatility, but from his reaction to it. Not to mention we no longer work together. Sarah, on the other hand, stuck with her plan. Her dividends grew and her portfolio recovered from any dips, often stronger than before. By staying calm and focusing on the long term, Sarah took advantage of the same volatility that sent Mark into a spiral.

Both Mark and Sarah started in similar positions, but their approaches led them down very different paths. It just goes to show:

he way you respond to the market can be more important than the market itself.

YOUR BRAIN'S WORST ENEMY: ITSELF

You know that little voice in your head that tells you to eat the extra slice of pizza even though you're already full? Or the one that insists you check your phone one last time before bed, leading to a midnight scroll through social media? That's your brain, doing its thing—not always in your best interest.

Our brains are incredible machines, developed to keep us alive in a world filled with perils like saber-toothed tigers and suspicious-looking berries. They're wired to prioritize short-term survival over long-term benefits. Back in the day, if you heard a rustling in the bushes, your brain didn't wait around to consider the possibilities—your brain screamed, "Run!"

This fight-or-flight response was great for dodging predators, but it's a bit of a mismatch when it comes to modern challenges like, say, stock market volatility, when patience and perseverance are required.

Consider:

- **Fight or Flight:** In investing, this translates to "buy or sell." When fear takes over, the default reaction is to sell, eliminating the perceived threat. But in the stock market, the threat is often temporary volatility, not a permanent loss.
- **Loss Aversion:** We feel the pain of losses more acutely than the pleasure of gains. This can lead to irrational decisions, like selling investments at a loss to prevent potential further losses, even when holding could cause recovery and profit.
- **Herd Mentality:** If everyone else is selling, shouldn't you? Our brains love the safety of the crowd, but following the herd can lead you off a cliff—financially speaking.

THE PSYCHOLOGY BEHIND PANIC SELLING

Let's go back to that phone alert from the start of the chapter: "Market Plunges Amid Global Uncertainty!" While your heart pounds and palms sweat, your mind, ever the drama queen, starts playing a disaster reel of your financial future—retirement plans evaporating, forced to live off ramen noodles in your golden years, the whole nine yards.

This is your amygdala at work—the ancient part of your brain responsible for processing emotions like fear and anxiety. It's the same part that would have helped you sprint away from that saber-toothed tiger. In investing, however, it's more like a smoke alarm that goes off every time you make toast—annoying and not particularly helpful.

When the market takes a dip, your amygdala screams, "Get out now! Save yourself!" And many people listen, selling off their investments in a panic. This knee-jerk reaction might provide temporary relief, like scratching an itch, but often leads to long-term regret.

THE DANGER OF EMOTIONAL DECISIONS: A LESSON IN PATIENCE

Here's another story from early in my career. A client named Mike taught me a valuable lesson about the dangers of reacting emotionally to the market.

Mike was your everyday guy, solid job, family man, but when it came to his investments, he carried a bit more anxiety than most. Anytime the market wobbled, Mike's stress levels would skyrocket; he would often get consumed by what was happening. He'd check his portfolio obsessively, and every bad headline had him on edge. It wasn't long before things took a downturn—one of those inevitable market corrections that felt like the end of the world to many.

I remember sitting down with Mike one afternoon as he stared at his portfolio, watching the value slowly shrink day after day. The news was grim, and the pressure was mounting. Mike was on high alert, and his gut reaction was to get out. He felt like the market was going to swallow his savings whole if he didn't act fast.

One night, after a particularly rough day in the market, Mike made the call. It was late, and the panic was real. He sold off all his stocks, convinced it was the only way to avoid further losses. For a brief moment, he felt relief. His brain told him he'd done the right thing—that he had saved himself from disaster. The year was 2002.

Here's the part we all know too well: Not long after Mike sold everything, the market made a rebound. And it didn't just recover—it surged for seven straight years. While his cash sat idly by, stocks soared to new heights. By the time Mike felt comfortable getting back into the market, prices were much higher than when he sold, and his losses were already locked in. He didn't just miss the bounce back, he missed the next surge that could have not only repaired the damage but put him way ahead.

Mike had been trying to protect himself, but in doing so, he'd sabotaged his long-term goals. It's like deciding to quit a marathon at mile twenty because you're tired—you may get some immediate relief, but you miss out on the satisfaction of crossing the finish line. And in Mike's case, that finish line was a financial stability he'd been so close to achieving had he just held steady.

It's a situation I'll never forget, and it's one I've shared with many clients since—because sometimes the toughest part of investing isn't the market itself, but overcoming our own instincts.

HOW TO OUTSMART YOUR BRAIN

What's an investor to do? How can you keep your brain's well-intentioned but misguided instincts from derailing your financial future?

- **Acknowledge the Emotion:** First, recognize that feeling anxious during market downturns is normal. It's your brain doing what it's designed to do. Give yourself a mental pat on the back for caring about your financial well-being.

- **Pause Before Acting:** Implement a "cooling-off" period. Before making any drastic decisions, wait twenty-four hours. Often, the urge to react on an impulse will diminish, and you can make a more rational choice.
- **Focus on the Long Term:** Remind yourself of your investment goals and time horizon. If you're investing for retirement twenty years down the line, a short-term market dip is just a blip on the radar.
- **Revisit Your Investment Plan:** Ensure that your portfolio has strong companies with strong financials and aligned with your income needs. A well-constructed plan can provide reassurance during turbulent times.
- **Avoid Constant Monitoring:** Checking your portfolio every hour is a surefire way to feed your anxiety. Set regular, less frequent times to review your investments.

You can also counter your brain biases with the help of mindfulness techniques. Take a deep breath, step back, and review your investment philosophy. Are the companies you've invested in fundamentally sound? If yes, then hold steady. Remember, dividends provide income even when stock prices fluctuate.

THE TORTOISE, THE HARE, AND THE WISE OWL

To help drive home this point about patience, I'd like to share an old favorite storytelling device. Once upon a market cycle, a hare bragged about his high-flying growth stocks. "Look at my returns!" he boasted. The tortoise, with his modest dividend stocks, smiled but said nothing. The wise owl observed silently.

When the market turned south, the hare's portfolio plummeted.

Desperate, he sold his stocks at a loss. The tortoise's portfolio dipped too, but his dividends kept rolling in. He reinvested them, buying more shares at lower prices.

The owl finally spoke: "Fast gains often fade, but steady income prevails." The tortoise nodded, understanding that his patience and discipline paid off.

RISK MANAGEMENT: NOT ALL EGGS, NOT ONE BASKET

We've all heard the saying, "Don't put all your eggs in one basket." Yet, some investors go all in on the latest hot stock tip like it's the secret to eternal youth.

DIVERSIFICATION: THE FREE LUNCH OF INVESTING

Diversification involves spreading your investments across various sectors, industries, and asset classes. It's like a well-balanced diet for your portfolio—ensuring that a downturn in one area doesn't ruin your entire financial health.

However, Warren Buffett famously said, "Diversification is for those that don't know what they are doing." Now, I am not saying you shouldn't be diversifying your portfolio, but I am saying you shouldn't be diversified for diversification's sake.

THE ISLAND OF MISFIT STOCKS

Imagine owning stocks only in tech companies right before the dot-com bubble burst in 2000. Ouch. However, if you had a diversified portfolio that included dividend-paying stocks from utilities, consumer staples, and healthcare, the blow would have been softened greatly.

THE 60/40 PORTFOLIO IS SO LAST CENTURY

Traditional wisdom suggests a 60 percent stocks and 40 percent bonds portfolio. But with bond yields lower than a limbo stick at a Caribbean dance-off, it's time to rethink.

DIVIDEND GROWTH IS THE NEW BLACK

Dividend-growth investing can serve as both the growth and income portion of your portfolio. Companies that consistently increase dividends often have strong financials, providing growth potential and income streams.

THE HYBRID APPROACH

By focusing on dividend-paying stocks, you're not reliant on capital appreciation. The dividends provide a cushion during downturns, reducing the need to sell assets at unfavorable prices.

MARKET TIMING: THE UNICORN OF INVESTING STRATEGIES

Trying to time the market is like trying to catch a unicorn while blindfolded. Good luck with that.

Studies show that missing just a few of the market's best days can drastically reduce your returns. But those best days often occur during volatile times when most investors are on the sidelines.

Market prognosticators are about as reliable as weather forecasters. They have a 50 percent chance of being right. Instead of attempting to predict, focus on what you can control: your reactions.

EMOTIONAL DISCIPLINE: THE STOIC INVESTOR'S SECRET WEAPON

Emotional discipline isn't about suppressing feelings; it's about acknowledging them and not letting them dictate your actions. Here's a refresher of a few investing techniques I shared earlier; they can help you keep calm and carry on:

- **Set Clear Goals:** I wrote about this earlier. Key point: Knowing your investment objectives helps you stay focused.
- **Automate Investments:** Use automatic dividend reinvestment plans (DRIPs) to remove decision paralysis.
- **Regular Reviews, Not Obsessions:** Check your portfolio occasionally, not daily. Obsessive monitoring can lead to impulsive actions.
- **The Power of a Support System:** Sometimes, talking to a financial advisor or joining an investment community can provide perspective and reassurance. It's like having a gym buddy for your financial fitness.

THE EMOTIONAL BENEFITS OF DIVIDEND INVESTING

Beyond the numbers, dividend investing offers psychological comfort. Regular dividend payments can reduce anxiety during market downturns. It's easier to weather a storm when you have a steady supply of hot cocoa and marshmallows—or in this case, cash dividends.

Seeing consistent returns encourages you to stick to your plan. It's like getting a pat on the back from your investments, saying, "You're doing great; keep it up!"

In the end, investing shouldn't feel like you're trapped in a fun house of distorted mirrors and surprise pitfalls…as long as you:

- **Understand Risk:** Recognize that risk is both a financial and emotional concept.
- **Embrace Volatility:** Accept that it's part of the journey and can present opportunities.
- **Practice Emotional Discipline:** Control your reactions to market events.
- **Diversify:** Spread your investments to manage risk.
- **Focus on Dividends:** Let consistent cash flow be your anchor.

This reminds me of yet another fishing anecdote. A seasoned fisherman was teaching his apprentice how to navigate rough seas. "When the waves get big, do you fight them?" the apprentice asked.

"No," the fisherman replied. "You adjust your sails and ride them out."

Dividend-growth investing is about adjusting your financial sails to navigate the market's unpredictable waves. By focusing on long-term goals, managing risk, and maintaining emotional stability, you can sail smoothly, even when the seas get rough.

Now that we've navigated the ups and downs of risk management and emotional stability, it's time to look forward to how the seeds you plant today can grow into a lasting legacy for your family and beyond. In the next chapter, we'll dive deep into the world of dividend yield and explore how consistent, growing dividends can transform your wealth over time.

CHAPTER 8

Dividend Yield and Your Legacy

How Planting Financial Seeds Today Grows Money Trees Tomorrow

You know that moment when you're assembling a piece of IKEA furniture, and you wonder, "Is this one tiny screw holding the entire contraption together?" You might be tempted to see if it can be built without it because it's small and seems insignificant, but without it, the whole thing collapses faster than a house of cards in a wind tunnel.

In the grand scheme of investing, that tiny screw is your dividend yield. It might not seem like much at first glance, but over time, it's the linchpin that holds your financial future together.

In this chapter, we're diving deep into the magical world of yield and compounding—the dynamic duo that's less "Batman and Robin" and more "mac and cheese" of the investing universe. We'll explore how these concepts can help you not just feather your nest but build a legacy that would make your great-grandkids toast to your portrait above the fireplace.

YIELD: THE OAK TREE THAT OUTLASTS THE STORM

Let's start with yield—not the traffic sign that everyone ignores, but the portion of your investment that pays you back in cold, hard cash, also known as dividends. Think of yield as the unsung hero of your portfolio, quietly doing its job while the flashy stocks hog the spotlight.

THE CROCK-POT INVESTOR

Meet Bob. He's the guy who uses a slow cooker for his meals. He throws in the ingredients in the morning and comes home to a delicious dinner. No fuss, no constant checking, just set it and forget it.

Bob applies the same philosophy to investing. He buys stocks with solid dividend yields and lets them simmer over time. His neighbor, Flashy Frank, laughs at him. Frank is all about the latest stock tips, day trading, and enough screen time to make an optometrist cringe.

Years go by, and Bob's portfolio grows steadily. He's not making headlines, but his wealth is compounding. Frank, on the other hand, has developed an ulcer and a twitch from all the market volatility.

One day, Frank scoffs at Bob, "How's that Crock-pot portfolio treating you?"

Bob smiles and says, "Well, my dividends just paid for a two-week cruise. How about you?"

Frank mumbles something about market fluctuations and shuffles away.

The moral? Sometimes slow and steady not only wins the race but enjoys the journey along the way.

Please don't just gloss over this story and think to yourself, "I would never be Flashy Frank. Even the most seasoned and patient dividend investors have given into the desire to turn a quick profit. Unfortunately, Flashy Frank is in all of us.

THE MAGIC OF COMPOUNDING: YOUR MONEY MAKING MONEY BABIES

Compounding may not always get the spotlight it deserves, but its power is undeniable. It's like planting a single redwood seed. Over time, that seed grows into a towering tree, and before you know it, you've created a redwood forest, standing tall and resilient, just like dividends that grow stronger with each passing year.

FROM A DOLLAR TIP TO OWNING THE COFFEE SHOP

Imagine you're at a coffee shop, and you decide to put a dollar in the tip jar. The barista, grateful for your generosity, tells you about a special deal: Every day you come back, she'll double your tip amount in free coffee.

- **Day one:** You get $1 worth of coffee.
- **Day two:** $2 worth.
- **Day three:** $4 worth.

And so on. By day ten, you'd be getting $512 worth of coffee! By day twenty, you'd own the coffee shop. That's compounding in action. Okay, so maybe coffee shops don't offer that deal (I've asked), but the principle applies to your investments. Reinvesting your dividends creates a compounding effect that can turn modest returns into a financial avalanche over time.

PLANTING SEEDS TODAY FOR SHADE TOMORROW

Now, let's talk about legacy. Not the kind that gets you a building named after you—though, hey, aim high—but the kind that provides financial security for generations.

To help illustrate some points, I'll bring my father-in-law, Pops, into the mix. Pops is known for two things: fixing anything broken, and being resourceful. He doesn't believe in wasting time or tools. Every time he has a little extra, he'll buy a new tool for his collection, no matter how small or simple. Over the years, that modest toolbox grew into a complete workshop that could handle any job in the neighborhood.

Someday when he retires, he'll pass his entire workshop down to the family. What he loves as a useful hobby turned into an asset that will keep providing long after he hangs up his work boots. Pops won't just leave us tools; he will leave us the ability to build something lasting.

Investing in dividend-paying stocks is like building that toolbox. Each stock might seem small today, but over time, they can turn into a collection that provides for your family's future and keeps working for generations.

THE TIME FACTOR: YOUR BEST FRIEND AND WORST ENEMY

Time can be like that friend who's brutally honest. It won't sugarcoat things, but if you respect it, it'll reward you.

We live in a world obsessed with instant gratification. Microwave meals, binge-watching entire seasons, and same-day deliveries. But for building wealth, patience isn't just a virtue; it's a necessity.

Consider this: If you had invested $10,000 in Altria Group (MO) about thirty years ago, when the dividend yield was about 6 percent, and you reinvested those dividends, your investment would have grown significantly. By today, that $10,000 investment would be worth over $474,000, without adding a single extra penny. Even more impressive, the annual dividend payments today would be around $38,000, providing substantial income from your original investment. That's the power of time, compounding, and reinvesting dividends.

For building wealth, compounding is like having a long-term partner who does most of the heavy lifting over time.

Now, let's break it down even further. If you had invested that $10,000 in Altria Group (MO) thirty years ago and reinvested the dividends, you wouldn't just have a higher total portfolio value—you'd also own significantly more shares. Back then, Altria's stock price was around twenty-four dollars per share, meaning your initial $10,000 would have bought you about 415 shares. With the power of dividend reinvestment and compounding, those dividends would have purchased additional shares over the years, significantly increasing your share count. Today, instead of holding the original 415 shares, you'd likely be sitting on roughly 9,308 shares, thanks to the reinvestment of dividends. And with today's dividend payout of approximately $4.08 per share, those 9,308 shares would be generating a yearly dividend income of around $37,976—all from that original $10,000 investment. That's the power of compounding in action!

Now, let's say you didn't reinvest the dividends but collected them over time. If you had invested $10,000 in Altria Group (MO) thirty years ago and just held onto the stock, your investment would still be worth around $81,000 today. On top of that, you would have received tens of thousands of dollars in dividends over the years, providing a steady stream of income. Even without reinvesting, the power of holding dividend-paying stocks like MO can still offer significant growth and reliable income.

To wrap this up, let's contrast this with a typical growth stock. If you invested $10,000 in a growth stock that appreciated to $81,000 over thirty years, you'd see the value increase but without the added benefit of regular dividends. While growth stocks rely solely on price appreciation, dividend stocks like Altria provide both capital growth and income along the way.

With dividends, you have the flexibility to reinvest and supercharge your returns to $474,000, or simply collect a steady stream of cash over the years, which can add up to tens of thousands of dollars. In comparison, the growth stock may look similar at face value, but it lacks the dual advantage of immediate income and compounded growth—leaving dividend stocks as a more versatile wealth-building tool.

OVERCOMING THE LURE OF QUICK WINS

By now, you know I love fishing analogies. Here's another: going after quick wins is like a fisherman chasing a flashy lure. It looks tempting, glistening on the water, promising a quick and easy catch. But more often than not, it leads to an empty net.

In today's world, those lures are the latest hot stock tips and get-rich-quick schemes that sparkle in the moment but rarely deliver lasting success. Instead of chasing the shiny bait, focus on the steady, reliable approach that leads to real, long-term results.

THE LOTTERY TICKET ILLUSION

Playing the lottery is fun. The odds of winning? About one in three hundred million. Yet, people spend money on tickets every day, dreaming of instant wealth. Investing in speculative stocks with the hope of striking it rich is similar. Sure, someone hits the jackpot, but for most, it's a losing game.

Dividend investing requires discipline to resist these temptations. It's about embracing the "get rich slow" scheme—far less exciting at parties, but infinitely more rewarding in the long run.

TEACHING THE NEXT GENERATION: A FAMILY AFFAIR

Schools typically do not teach financial literacy, which is baffling given its importance. Passing on your knowledge can be just as valuable as the money itself.

Let me tell you about an awesome client of mine, Dave, and how he made investing a family affair. Dave had always been passionate about teaching his kids the importance of financial literacy, but he didn't just want to talk about it—he wanted to make it part of their everyday lives. So, one evening over dinner, he suggested they start a family investment club. Everyone was on board, and soon, their monthly meetings became a tradition.

At first, the kids were more interested in investing in companies they knew, like the ones that made video games or their favorite snack brands. Dave didn't mind. He saw it as an opportunity to introduce them to the basics of how dividends worked and the magic of compounding.

As the months turned into years, something incredible happened. The kids went from picking stocks based on what they liked to asking questions about dividend growth, balance sheets, and market trends. By the time they hit high school, they had real portfolios funded by their allowances, birthday money, and part-time jobs.

Dave didn't just help them build their financial futures—he built a family culture around understanding and managing money. Now, they don't just talk about the next family vacation or school events at the dinner table; they chat about their dividend stocks and future financial goals. It's amazing to see how something that started with a few simple lessons has turned into lifelong financial confidence for his kids.

THE PSYCHOLOGICAL PAYOFF: PEACE OF MIND AND PURPOSE

Let's be honest: While money can't buy happiness, it can certainly purchase a more comfortable brand of misery. Beyond the spreadsheets, charts, and the thrill of watching your investments grow, there's a less tangible but equally important benefit to savvy financial planning: the psychological payoff. It's that warm, fuzzy feeling you get from knowing your financial house is in order, like the satisfaction of finding a match for every lid in your Tupperware collection.

Remember when you were a kid, and you'd build a pillow fort, convinced it was impenetrable? Inside that cozy fortress, nothing could touch you—not monsters, not thunderstorms, not even your sibling's annoying habits. That's the peace of mind a solid financial plan can provide in adulthood.

THE INVISIBLE ROI: RETURN ON INNER PEACE

We often focus on ROI in terms of dollars and percentages, but what about the return on inner peace? Financial stability reduces stress, which isn't just good for your mood—it's good for your health. Lower stress levels can lead to better sleep, reduced risk of chronic illnesses, and even improved relationships (because who hasn't snapped at a loved one when stressed about money?).

LEAVING A FOOTPRINT

We all want to be remembered. Building a financial legacy allows you to leave a positive mark, whether it's ensuring your family's security or contributing to causes you care about. It's the financial equivalent of planting trees under whose shade you'll never sit.

A CHERISHED NOTE

When my grandpa passed away in the mid-nineties, he left me some money and a note. While the money was great, especially as a teenager, the note is far more valuable to me. He wrote down all the things he never wanted me to forget, something I will always cherish. To be honest, I have no idea what I spent the money on that he left me, but I know exactly where that note is located and what it says.

FINANCIAL LEGACIES ARE THE NEW FAMILY RECIPES

Investing and building wealth can be like planting that garden. You're not just accumulating money; you're cultivating resources and values that can benefit others long after you're gone. Whether it's paying for a child's education, supporting a charitable cause, or providing financial security for your family, your investments can have a ripple effect.

The Ripple Effect of Generosity

Consider philanthropists like Warren Buffett and Bill Gates. They've amassed wealth not just for personal gain, but to make significant contributions to society. While we might not all have billions to give away, even minor acts of financial generosity can leave a lasting impact.

- **Scholarship Funds:** Setting up a small scholarship can change the trajectory of someone's life.
- **Community Investments:** Funding local projects can improve neighborhoods and create a sense of pride and belonging.
- **Family Support:** Helping family members start a business or buy their first home can set them on a path to success.

THE EMOTIONAL DIVIDEND: MORE THAN JUST FINANCIAL RETURNS

CONFIDENCE IN DECISION-MAKING

When you understand your finances and have a plan in place, you make decisions from a position of strength rather than fear. This confidence spills over into other areas of life: career choices, personal relationships, even your willingness to try new things.

REDUCING FINANCIAL ANXIETY

Money is one of the leading causes of stress. By taking control of your financial future, you're effectively telling that stress, "Not today, pal." Lower anxiety means more mental capacity for the things you love, whether it's hobbies, family time, or finally mastering the ukulele.

BEATING INFLATION (THE SILENT WEALTH ASSASSIN)

Ignoring inflation is like trying to run on a treadmill that's slowly speeding up—you may be moving, but you're not getting ahead.

Inflation erodes purchasing power. What costs a dollar today might cost two dollars in the future. Dividend growth stocks can help combat this. Companies that regularly increase their dividends often do so at a rate that outpaces inflation.

For example, if a company increases its dividend by 5 percent annually, and inflation is at 2 percent, your actual income is still growing. Reinvesting those dividends amplifies the effect, helping you stay ahead of the inflation monster.

THE LONG GAME WINS

Here's what we've learned on this enlightening journey:

- **Yield Is Your Friend:** Don't underestimate the power of a modest dividend yield. Over time, it packs a punch.
- **Compounding Is Magical:** Reinvesting dividends creates a snowball effect that can lead to substantial wealth.
- **Legacy Matters:** Investing isn't just about you; it's about the impact you can have on future generations.
- **Time Is a Critical Factor:** The earlier you start, the more powerful the effects of compounding.
- **Avoid Short-Term Temptations:** Stick to your long-term plan and avoid the siren calls of quick gains.
- **Educate the Next Generation:** Pass on your knowledge to empower your family.
- **Psychological Benefits Are Real:** Peace of mind and a sense of purpose are invaluable.
- **Beat Inflation:** Dividend growth can help you outpace inflation.

As we wrap up this chapter, let me tell you about a client named Thomas—by no means a Wall Street hotshot. Thomas drove a city garbage truck, hopping on and off the back to empty cans along endless suburban streets. His pay never cracked thirty-five grand a year, and the job was more "early-morning diesel fumes" than corner-office glamour.

Yet every month, Thomas carved out a sliver of that modest paycheck and sent it straight into dividend-paying stocks. He skipped gadgets, packed his own lunches, and found joy in fishing on Saturdays instead of fancy vacations.

When Thomas passed away, his family asked me to help settle his estate—and they nearly fell over when they saw the numbers. Decades of steady dividend reinvestment had snowballed into a small fortune that kept throwing off income for his children and even his grandkids. Thomas, the quiet sanitation worker, didn't just haul away trash for a living; he quietly carted home a legacy that will keep paying out long after the last garbage route with his name on it.

His family used the wealth to fund their children's children's college tuition, start businesses, and support ministries that were near and dear to their family. Thomas's legacy wasn't just the money, but the opportunities it created.

What about your legacy? You don't need to be a financial wizard or inherit a fortune to build wealth and create a legacy. All it takes is discipline, patience, and a commitment to the long game. Start planting your financial seeds today. Reinvest those dividends, educate yourself and your family, and watch as your modest garden grows into an orchard. Remember, the best time to plant a tree was twenty years ago. The second-best time is now.

On that note, we're about to switch gears in the next chapter and focus on the emotional roller coaster that can derail even the best-laid financial plans. To do so, we'll dive even deeper into the psychological battleground of greed and fear—two of the biggest drivers behind poor investing decisions. Better yet, the next chapter will arm you with the tools of what I call rational investing.

CHAPTER 9

Greed, Fear, and Rational Investing

How Not to Let Your Inner Drama Queen Ruin Your Financial Future

You know that moment when you're at an all-you-can-eat buffet and your eyes scan the endless options? Before you know it, your plate is piled high with sushi, lasagna, fried chicken, and maybe a waffle for good measure. Halfway through, you realize you've overcommitted, but hey, you don't want to waste food—or admit defeat. That's greed, my friends. It's your appetite convincing you that you can handle more than you actually can.

Now, imagine the flip side. You're at the same buffet, but this time you've heard rumors about questionable kitchen hygiene. Suddenly, even the salad looks suspect. You pick at a dry bread roll, eyeing the exits in case you need to make a swift getaway. That's fear. It's that gnawing sensation that maybe, just maybe, you should sit this one out.

In the grand buffet of the stock market, greed and fear are the overzealous servers dishing out heaping portions of emotional turmoil.

In this chapter, we're going to explore how these two troublemakers can wreak havoc on your investment decisions, and how a steady diet of rational, dividend-focused investing can keep you healthy and satisfied.

GREED: THE SIREN SONG OF SUDDEN WEALTH

Let's dive into greed first—the alluring whisper that says, "You could double your money overnight!" It's like the late-night infomercial promising six-pack abs with just three minutes of exercise a day while eating whatever you want. You know deep down it's too good to be true, but imagine if it actually was.

THE MIRAGE OF CERTAINTY

Meet Steve, a seasoned investor and soon-to-be client of mine with a long track record of smart financial moves.

One day, Steve stumbled upon an investment in a medical supply company that seemed like a no-brainer. With the global demand for healthcare on the rise, this opportunity seemed as close to "low risk" as you could get—at least, that's how Steve described it. The catch? It was for accredited investors only, meaning Steve had to acknowledge that he could afford to lose his entire investment if things went sideways.

Confident this medical supply company was poised to skyrocket, Steve invested a significant portion of his portfolio in the venture. After all, medical supplies seemed like a safe bet—people will always need them, right? For a while, everything appeared to progress. The investment climbed, and Steve started imagining a nice early retirement funded by this "sure thing."

But then the unexpected happened. The company ran into regulatory issues, delaying their key product launches. To make matters worse, a major competitor entered the market with a more innovative solution, pulling the rug out from under the medical supply firm. The investment that seemed so "safe" quickly spiraled downward, and Steve's hefty stake evaporated.

The moral: Steve's belief in the "low risk" nature of the investment clouded his judgment. While the opportunity appeared straightforward, he overlooked the fact that investing in private, high-stakes ventures—especially those limited to accredited investors—came with real risks, no matter how solid they seemed. By putting too much faith in one venture, Steve learned the hard way that diversification and due diligence are critical, even in industries that seem bulletproof.

FEAR: THE PARALYZING PHANTOM

Now let's chat about fear—the voice in your head that whispers, "The sky is falling!" It's like that friend who forwards you conspiracy theories and insists that tap water is turning frogs into amateur magicians. Fear can be irrational, but it feels so real.

Meet Pam. She's the person who checks the weather forecast every hour. Just in case. When it comes to investing, she's equally cautious. After finally deciding to dip her toes into the market, she bought shares in a solid, dividend-paying company.

Then, a news headline screamed about a market correction with no end in sight. Stocks dropped by 5 percent, and Pam spiraled. She envisioned economic collapse, packed an emergency go bag, and sold all her stocks at a loss. Two weeks later, the market recovered, her former stock reached an all-time high, and Pam was left holding nothing but canned beans and regret.

The moral: Fear drove Pam to make a hasty decision, causing her to realize losses that could have been temporary on paper.

THE EMOTIONAL ROLLER COASTER: RIDING THE MARKET'S WILD SWINGS

Investing can feel like being strapped into a roller coaster designed by a maniac with a flair for the dramatic. One moment you're climbing to exhilarating heights; the next, you're plunging into stomach-churning lows. The trick isn't to avoid the ride, but to manage how you react to it.

UNDERSTANDING LOSS AVERSION

Psychologists have found that we feel the pain of loss about twice as much as the pleasure of an equivalent gain.[15] It's why losing fifty dollars feels like a punch in the gut, but finding fifty dollars is just mildly exciting. This quirk in our brain chemistry can lead to irrational decisions, like selling off investments at the first sign of trouble or chasing risky ventures to recoup losses.

Imagine this: You're playing a game at the fair. You've won a giant teddy bear and are feeling good about it. Then, you lose ten dollars on a rigged ring toss and spend the rest of the night obsessing over that lost ten dollars, completely forgetting about the teddy bear you're lugging around. That's loss aversion in a nutshell.

RATIONAL INVESTING: THE CALM IN THE STORM

How do we keep greed and fear from turning us into financial basket cases? The answer lies in rational investing—making decisions based on logic, research, and a long-term perspective rather than emotional reactions.

15 Daniel Kahneman and Amos Tversky, "Prospect Theory: An Analysis of Decision Under Risk," *Econometrica* 47, no. 2 (March 1979), https://doi.org/10.2307/1914185.

STICK TO FUNDAMENTALS

Invest in companies with strong financial health, consistent earnings, and a history of paying dividends. These anchors of the market—the blue-chip stocks—focus on steady growth, rather than chasing the latest fad. Think of it like dating. Would you rather be with someone reliable and supportive, or someone who's exciting but unpredictable? Your portfolio deserves a partner it can count on.

DIVERSIFY LIKE A BUFFET, BUT SMARTER

While greed might tempt you to load up on one hot stock, diversification spreads your risk across different sectors and asset classes. It's like going to that buffet and taking a little bit of everything (except the questionable sushi). This way, if one investment gives you indigestion, the others can keep your portfolio healthy.

Think of each investment as a different food group. If one doesn't sit well—say, the tech sector gets a case of market food poisoning—your other "food groups" can keep your portfolio nourished. It's like having an antacid ready after that extra serving of spicy chili. You're prepared for the discomfort.

With good insights and understanding, at times it's okay to stack your plate with more of one food group. Again, don't diversify for diversification's sake.

IGNORE THE NOISE

Financial news outlets can be like that overcaffeinated friend who texts you at 3:00 a.m. about the latest drama—more stress than they're worth. Markets will fluctuate; that's their nature. Obsessing over every dip and spike is as productive as checking your fridge every ten minutes to see if new food has appeared (not that I know anything about this).

Here are tips to tuning out the noise:

- **Set It and Forget It:** Once you've established your investment strategy, stick to it. Rebalance periodically, but avoid knee-jerk reactions to every market hiccup.
- **Limit Media Consumption:** Designate specific times to catch up on financial news and consider focusing on reputable sources rather than sensationalist headlines.
- **Trust the Process:** Remember why you invested in the first place. If your investments are sound, short-term volatility shouldn't derail your long-term goals.
- **Find a Hobby:** Whether it's knitting, kayaking, or learning the harmonica, keeping busy with activities you enjoy can distract you from unnecessary worrying.

THE PRODUCTIVITY BLACK HOLE

Markets naturally fluctuate. They're influenced by countless factors, from economic data to tweets from eccentric billionaires. Obsessing over every tiny movement is not only exhausting but can lead to impulsive decisions that hurt your long-term financial health.

REINVESTING DIVIDENDS: THE DOMINO EFFECT

Reinvesting your dividends is like setting off a chain reaction with a line of dominoes. Instead of pocketing those quarterly payouts for a quick treat, you use them to buy more shares. Each new share earns its own dividends, setting off the next "domino" in the sequence.

Over time, this domino effect grows. Each payout leads to more shares and more payouts, building momentum with every cycle. What begins as a small nudge can snowball into something much bigger, with your investments doing the hard work while you sit back and enjoy the long-term growth.

GRACE GRONER'S INCREDIBLE PATIENCE PAYS OFF

Let's talk about Grace Groner, whose story is a real-life testament to the power of patience, dividend reinvestment, and long-term investing.

Grace was a secretary at Abbott Laboratories, a job she started in 1935. She wasn't wealthy by any stretch of the imagination. In 1935, she bought three shares of Abbott stock for $180.[16] And here's the kicker—she never sold them. Instead, she reinvested every dividend the company paid out over the decades to follow.

By the time she passed away in 2010, Grace's modest investment had grown to over seven million dollars, all thanks to the power of compounding and reinvesting dividends. Even though she lived simply throughout her life, she amassed an incredible fortune without any big market plays or fancy trading tactics. The dividends and stock growth were so significant that she left her entire fortune to a charitable foundation that supports students at her alma mater, Lake Forest College.

Grace's story is a powerful example of how small, consistent investments and dividend reinvestment can transform into financial security and wealth over time—without chasing market trends or stressing over the day-to-day fluctuations.

---

16 John Keilman, "Secret Millionaire Donates Fortune to Lake Forest College," *Chicago Tribune*, March 5, 2010, https://www.chicagotribune.com/2010/03/05/secret-millionaire-donates-fortune-to-lake-forest-college-2/.

THE INVESTOR WHO STAYED THE COURSE

Let's talk about Jim and dig into his journey. Jim began investing in the 1980s. He witnessed Black Monday in 1987, the Dot-Com Bubble, the 2008 Financial Crisis, and the 2020 pandemic-induced market crash. Each time, he felt the same gut-wrenching anxiety anyone would have. But instead of giving in to fear, Jim held onto his diversified, dividend-paying stocks.

During downturns, he didn't just sit tight; he bought more shares at lower prices, boosting his future dividend income. When others saw the disaster, Jim saw a sale. His mantra was always the same: "Markets recover, but lost opportunities don't." By staying the course, he benefited from the market's long-term upward trajectory.

GREED AND FEAR ARE NOT YOUR FINANCIAL ADVISORS

It's important to recognize that both greed and fear are natural human emotions. They're great for survival (like avoiding bears or not eating that questionable sushi) but terrible for investing.

Here are some practical tips to help you keep emotions in check:

- **Set Clear Goals:** Know why you're investing. Retirement? College fund? Yacht named Seas the Day? Having clear objectives helps you stay focused.
- **Automate Investments:** Set up automatic contributions to your investment accounts. This removes the temptation to time the market.
- **Review, Don't Obsess:** Check your plan and portfolio periodically, not daily. Constant monitoring can lead to knee-jerk reactions.
- **Educate Yourself:** Knowledge is power. The more you understand about investing, the less likely you are to make decisions based on emotion.

BE THE MASTER OF YOUR FINANCIAL JOURNEY

At the end of the day, investing is a marathon, not a sprint. It's about making consistent, rational decisions and not letting short-term market fluctuations derail your long-term goals. Remember:

- **Greed and Fear Are Temporary; Your Goals Are Not:** Don't let fleeting emotions dictate your strategy.
- **Dividends Are Your Friends:** They provide income and can be reinvested to accelerate growth.
- **Stay the Course:** Markets will go up and down, but historically, they've trended upward over the long term.

The next time the market takes you on an emotional roller coaster, take a deep breath, maybe do some yoga, and remember that rational investing is your seat belt, airbag, and emergency brake all rolled into one.

And with that, it's time to barrel into our next chapter, where we'll tackle the powerhouse behind every solid dividend-paying company: free cash flow.

We'll break down how free cash flow acts as the fuel that powers not just dividend payments but also their growth. We'll also talk about spotting companies with strong free cash flow, recognizing red flags, and understanding why this metric is more reliable than earnings when assessing a company's financial health.

CHAPTER 10

The Free Cash Flow Advantage

How Free Cash Flow Is like Your Grandma's Secret Cookie Jar

Imagine you're back in high school, juggling homework and a part-time job while also maintaining some semblance of a social life. You've got a paycheck coming in from your job at the local pizza joint, but after you cover your gas, phone bill, and those new sneakers you just had to have, what's left? That's your free cash flow—FCF for those of you who love acronyms. FCF refers to the money you stash away, spend on concert tickets, or maybe even save for college. And let's be honest: You went to the concert and asked your parents to pay for college.

Now, scale FCF up to the global business world. Companies have revenues and expenses, just like you. After they pay their bills and invest in new projects, FCF is what they have left. And just like your leftover cash, companies use it for whatever they want.

WHY SHOULD YOU CARE ABOUT THEIR FREE CASH FLOW?

Let's start at the start. Free cash flow is the cash a company has left over after they take care of expenses and capital investments. Basically, after they "pay the rent, buy groceries, and fill the gas tank."

Why should you, as an investor, care about some company's free cash flow? Well, as I wrote above, this is the money they use to do things like:

1. Pay dividends and share the wealth with investors.
2. Buy back shares, which reduces the number of shares outstanding, making each share you own more valuable.
3. Reinvest in the business by funding new projects, research, and innovations.
4. Pay down debt, reduce liabilities, and strengthen their financial position.

In essence, free cash flow is the lifeblood of a company's financial health. It's the difference between a business that's just getting by and one that's thriving.

Here's where the magic happens. If a company consistently generates solid free cash flow, it has more flexibility to increase dividends over time. You, as a dividend investor, are banking on that. You're not just interested in getting paid today—you want your payments to grow year after year.

THE CASE OF THE HIGH-PROFILE CEO AND THE CASH FLOW CONUNDRUM

Jeff was the kind of client who made spreadsheets for fun. A C-suite veteran with a résumé full of bottom-line wins, he prided himself on letting data—not ego—call the shots. Then one Tuesday he bounded into my office grinning like he'd just found a winning lottery ticket.

"Paul, you have to look at this company," he said, sliding a glossy investor deck across my desk. "Derek's on the board." Derek was Jeff's golf-course buddy—also a well-known tech CEO and, in Jeff's eyes, the second coming of Steve Jobs. If Derek said the product was revolutionary, that was good enough for Jeff. Share price? Up 40 percent in three months. Media buzz? Off the charts. Due diligence? A casual fist-bump after the ninth hole.

The numbers, however, were a different story. Cash flow statements read like a campfire horror tale: negative free cash flow, ballooning R&D bills, and marketing spend that made Super Bowl advertisers look thrifty. They were torching cash faster than I could drain a Monday morning coffee. I asked, "Jeff, great narrative—but what's plan B if the rocket boosters fizzle?"

Silence. Then a nervous laugh. "Well, Derek says—"

"Right," I interrupted, "but Derek can't pay dividends with charisma. Without free cash flow, there's no safety net—no cushion for shareholders, no fuel for future growth, no paycheck for you if the story turns into a cautionary tale."

The spell broke. Jeff stepped back from his buddy's hype and redirected those dollars into companies that mint steady, positive free cash flow—businesses that can keep hiking dividends whether the market is doing backflips or face-plants.

Moral of the story: Friendships are priceless, but investment theses need more than a buddy's handshake. If a company can't convert hype into hard cash, you're betting on hope instead of holding something real.

Derek's "can't miss" rocket did keep climbing—for a good bit longer. Then the fuel gauge hit E, the stock nose-dived, and a larger tech giant scooped up the company for a sum rumored to be roughly equivalent to a well-used food truck and a year's supply of kombucha. Jeff still golfs with Derek, but he leaves the stock tips in the cart's cupholder—right next to the scorecard that says "double bogey."

THE DIFFERENCE BETWEEN EARNINGS AND FREE CASH FLOW (IT'S NOT WHAT YOU THINK)

You might be thinking, "Wait a minute. Don't I already know how profitable a company is by looking at its earnings?" That's a great question.

Here's the thing: Earnings and free cash flow are not the same. Earnings (or net income) are the profits a company reports on its income statement. Here's the kicker: Earnings can be manipulated. Yup, you heard that right.

Through accounting adjustments, companies can make their earnings look better than they actually are. Depreciation, stock-based compensation, amortization—these are all accounting tricks that can make a company's bottom line look prettier than reality.

Free cash flow, on the other hand, doesn't lie. It's actual cash in hand, and as the saying goes, "Cash is king." It's the cold, hard cash that a company can use to pay dividends, reinvest, or pay down debt. That's why dividend investors focus on free cash flow instead of just earnings. Free cash flow shows you a company's real financial health.

Analogy alert: Think of earnings as the frosting on a cake—it might look delicious, but if the cake underneath is dry and crumbly (i.e., poor cash flow), you're in for a disappointing dessert.

THE CEO WHO "LOOKED" PROFITABLE BUT HAD NO CASH

Let me tell you about another client, Susan, who came to me raving about some new stock she loved. They were reporting incredible earnings growth, and she was convinced it was a good buy. I'll admit, on the surface, the company looked fantastic. Their earnings were through the roof.

When I dug into their financials, something didn't add up. Their free cash flow was negative. All the "profits" they were reporting were tied up in noncash items like stock options they had issued to employees and the depreciation of assets. Sure, they were "profitable" on paper, but there wasn't any real cash coming in to pay investors or fuel long-term growth.

I explained to Susan that while earnings are important, free cash flow is the real star of the show. Without it, the company couldn't pay dividends, and if things got rough, they'd have no cushion to fall back on. Susan decided to stay the course with dividend-paying companies that had a history of generating positive free cash flow, and she's been thanking me ever since. Sure enough, years later that stock she once loved was acquired in a fire sale so cheap the buyers basically paid in expired Starbucks gift cards.

THE SWEET FRUIT OF FREE CASH FLOW

Remember when you were a kid, and your grandma had that secret cookie jar she only brought out on special occasions? Companies with strong free cash flow are like grandma's cookie jar—filled with a stash of goodies (cash) to share with you.

Dividends are paid out of free cash flow. If a company consistently generates more cash than it needs, it can reward shareholders by paying and increasing dividends. This is especially important for dividend growth investors who rely on those increasing payouts to fuel their own financial goals.

WHERE FREE CASH FLOW AND YOUR PAYCHECK MEET

Now that we've established the importance of free cash flow, let's talk about how it translates into dividends. Dividends are essentially your share of a company's free cash flow. If the company has a surplus of cash, it can share it with shareholders. If it doesn't, well…you're out of luck.

Let me give you an example: Imagine you own a small bakery. After you've paid for ingredients, rent, employee wages, and a new oven, whatever's left over is your profit (your free cash flow). Now, if business is booming and you're consistently generating more profit than you need, you can decide to pay yourself (and any partners) a nice chunk of that cash as a reward: your dividend.

That's exactly how companies work. The more free cash flow they generate, the more they can pay in dividends. And here's the best part: Companies with healthy free cash flow can increase those dividends over time. This is where dividend-growth investing shines. You're not just looking for a company that can pay you today; you want one that can keep increasing those payments year after year.

THE CLIENT WHO HAD IT HANDLED—EVEN WHEN THE MARKET DIDN'T

Dave was a dividend veteran long before he collected the sheet cake at his own retirement party. After thirty years of conference calls and corporate coffee, he clocked out for good, set his 6:00 a.m. alarm to *never*, and promoted himself to CEO of Tuesdays-on-the-golf-course. Then he literally flipped the switch in his brokerage account from "reinvest" to "payout," letting those responsible dividends start paying for tee times and grandkid ice-cream runs.

About a year later the market hiccupped—down nearly 15 percent in six weeks. Memories of an old client who'd spiraled during a crisis nudged me to pick up the phone. No way was I letting surprise sneak up on Dave.

"Thought I'd check in," I said, trying to sound casual. "Wild stretch out there. How are you holding up?"

Dave chuckled. "Paul, I've been retired thirteen months and the market's already thrown two tantrums. Stock prices are teenagers—they slam doors. My dividends are adults; they show up for work."

Still, I suggested coffee. I arrived with printouts, ready to walk him through the figures. Dave arrived with a grin and last quarter's income tally, which was already highlighted. Even after the pullback, his dividend line was up 6 percent year over year—better than the grocery-store inflation he'd been tracking on a Post-it at home.

"I watch the income column," he told me, tapping the page. "Prices bounce; paychecks climb. As long as this number keeps growing, the lights stay on and the grandkids stay sugared."

My concern melted quicker than his cappuccino foam. Dave didn't need reassurance; he *embodied* it. The market could keep slamming doors—his dividend stream was the grown-up in the house, quietly giving itself a raise while the price chart threw its fits.

HOW TO SPOT A COMPANY WITH STRONG FREE CASH FLOW

How do you know if a company is generating solid free cash flow? Here are a few things to look for:

1. **Consistent Cash Flow Generation:** Look for companies that have a track record of generating positive free cash flow over multiple years. One good year doesn't cut it—you want consistency.
2. **Low Debt Levels:** If a company has too much debt, they'll have to use their free cash flow to pay it down instead of sharing it with shareholders. A company with manageable debt levels has more flexibility to pay dividends.
3. **Dividend Payout Ratio:** This is the percentage of a company's free cash flow that is paid out as dividends. A payout ratio that's too high (think 90–100 percent) means the company might be stretching itself thin to pay dividends. A healthy payout ratio (typically 40–60 percent) means the company is generating enough cash to cover its dividends while still reinvesting in the business.

4. **Reinvestment Potential:** A company with solid free cash flow not only pays dividends but reinvests in growth opportunities. Look for companies that are using their cash to fund expansion, research, and development while still rewarding shareholders.

THE "TOO GOOD TO BE TRUE" COMPANY

Kevin was excited about a stock that seemed like a gold mine. The company was paying a massive dividend—way higher than the average. On the surface, it felt like a dream come true. Kevin came to me practically buzzing with excitement. He thought he'd found the holy grail of investing.

Here's the thing: When a company offers a dividend yield that's much higher than its peers, it's worth pausing to ask, "Why?" It's like that one pizza place that always has a buy-one-get-one deal. It sounds great, but you start wondering what's wrong with the pizza.

I took a look at the company's financials, and sure enough, their free cash flow was in the red. They were borrowing money to pay those high dividends, which is like using a credit card to pay your bills—sustainable for a bit, but eventually the house of cards collapses.

I explained to Kevin that while the high dividend looked tempting, it wasn't backed by healthy cash flow. It was, essentially, a ticking time bomb. Sure enough, a few months later, the company slashed its dividend, and the stock price took a nosedive. Kevin dodged a bullet by focusing on companies with strong, reliable free cash flow instead of chasing unsustainable high yields.

FREE CASH FLOW: THE LIFEBLOOD OF DIVIDEND GROWTH

At this point, you're probably starting to see the big picture. Free cash flow is the lifeblood of dividend-growth investing. It's what fuels those consistent, reliable dividends, and it's what allows companies to increase their payouts year after year.

Companies that generate strong free cash flow don't just survive during tough economic times—they thrive. They can continue paying and even increasing their dividends while others are cutting back. It's the ultimate sign of a financially healthy company, and as a dividend investor, it's your best friend.

What's the moral of the stories I've shared? Simple: Follow the cash. Free cash flow is the real indicator of a company's ability to pay you dividends—today, tomorrow, and in the future. Earnings can be manipulated, and stock prices can be volatile, but free cash flow doesn't lie.

As a dividend investor, you want to build a portfolio of companies that generate healthy free cash flow, have manageable debt, and use their cash to reward shareholders through dividends and reinvestment. If you focus on those companies, you'll set yourself up for long-term success.

And remember, the people in the stories I shared—Jeff, Susan, Dave, and Kevin—all learned valuable lessons about the importance of free cash flow.

- Jeff learned to step back from the hype.
- Susan realized that earnings don't always tell the whole story.
- Dave found a way to give himself a raise in retirement.
- Kevin avoided a high-yield disaster by focusing on financial fundamentals.

The next time you're looking at a potential investment, ask yourself: Does this company generate enough free cash flow to cover its dividends? If the answer is yes, you're on the right track. If the answer is no, it might be time to reconsider.

Keep your eyes on the cash, and you'll avoid a lot of the pitfalls that come with chasing short-term gains or following the latest market trends. Free cash flow is your compass in the investing world. It keeps you grounded and points you in the direction of long-term wealth.

With that, it's time to tackle the invisible enemy that's been silently eroding your purchasing power for decades: inflation. Don't worry. We're not just here to complain about rising prices. We'll dive into how dividend-growth investing can be your secret weapon against inflation. You'll see why rising dividends are more than just a paycheck. They're your shield against the "silent thief."

CHAPTER 11

The Inflation-Resistant Paycheck

How Dividend Growth Turns Inflation into Yesterday's News

Let's talk about inflation, that silent thief that sneaks into your wallet and makes everything more expensive. One day, you're buying a gallon of milk for $2.50. Next thing you know, it's $5 and you're wondering if cows have somehow unionized and demanded higher wages.

Inflation doesn't care about your grocery bill, your retirement plans, or that fancy dinner reservation you had in mind. It just keeps creeping up, quietly eating away at the value of your money.

Now, if you're like most people, inflation is that nagging worry at the back of your mind—especially when you're relying on investments to fund your retirement. But here's the good news: Dividend-growth investing is like a security system for your wallet. It's not going to stop inflation, but it can sure as heck protect your purchasing power against it.

In this chapter, we're going to dive into how dividend-growth investing acts as a hedge against inflation and why it's the financial equivalent of wearing sunscreen in the middle of a heat wave—it won't stop the heat, but it'll protect you from getting burned.

INFLATION: THE ULTIMATE PARTY CRASHER

First, let's define inflation in a way that doesn't make you want to doze off. Inflation is just the rise in prices over time. It's why movie tickets that used to cost five dollars are now fifteen dollars. It's why your grandparents' stories about how little they paid for gas sound like a wild fairy tale. It's that thing that makes your dollar today worth less tomorrow.

Let me give you a client example. A few years ago, I had a client named Linda. She was nearing retirement and came to me with a look of panic. "How am I supposed to retire when everything keeps getting more expensive? I'm worried that ten years from now, my money won't stretch far enough."

Linda's concern was real and something most of us can relate to. She wasn't just worried about her investments today—she was worried about what those investments would be worth in the future, especially with inflation eating away at her purchasing power.

That's where dividend-growth investing comes in.

Dividends act as an inflation fighter. You see, the beauty of dividend-growth investing is that it doesn't just give you income—*it gives you growing income*. And that's the key. When you invest in companies that consistently increase their dividends, you're essentially getting a built-in raise every year. It's like having a job where your boss surprises you with an annual pay bump, without you even asking.

I explained this to Linda. "Think of dividends as your paycheck in retirement. But instead of staying stagnant, that paycheck increases over time to keep up with the cost of living. It's like you're getting a raise every year just for sticking with the same companies."

Here's how it works in practice: Imagine you own stock in a company like Procter & Gamble (P&G). P&G has been increasing its dividend for decades. So while inflation might bump up the price of your groceries, P&G is simultaneously bumping up your dividend payments. That extra cash helps offset the rising costs, protecting your purchasing power. You're not just getting paid; you're getting paid more as time goes on.

FREE CASH FLOW: THE FUEL FOR DIVIDEND GROWTH

Let's get a little technical—I promise I'll keep it painless. You already know from the last chapter that free cash flow (FCF) is the lifeblood of dividend payments. Where FCF really shines is when headlines scream *inflation*, *recession*, or *market sell-off*. Companies swimming in free cash flow can still invest in growth, pay down debt, and—most importantly—keep raising dividends while everyone else is just trying to stay afloat.

THE "ON SALE" CONVERSATION WITH TOM

Tom, a longtime dividend devotee, rang me during a market swoon.

"Paul, two of my dividend stocks are down 15 percent. Maybe I should dump them before they sink further."

"Dump them?" I laughed. "Tom, you just walked into Costco and saw your favorite rib eyes at 15 percent off. Do you complain…or load the cart?"

"But prices might keep falling," he countered.

"Exactly—*might*. Meanwhile, those companies are still gushing free cash flow. Their dividend checks didn't shrink; the yield actually went up because the price went down. Reinvest those fatter dividends at the discount, and when the market sobers up, you'll own more shares *and* a bigger income stream."

Tom kept the stocks, reinvested every penny, and even added a little extra while they were "on sale." Five years later the share prices didn't just bounce back; they pulled a double backflip off a trampoline and stuck the landing. His dividend income was up nearly 50 percent, and he now roots for temporary dips the way kids beg for snow days—because free-cash-flow machines always plow the road clear again.

REINVESTING DIVIDENDS: COMPOUNDING YOUR PROTECTION

There's one more layer to inflation defense: **reinvesting your dividends**. Every time you plow those checks back into more shares, you turbocharge a snowball effect—more shares create more dividends, which buy even more shares, and so on. But the real magic shows up when you pair that reinvestment with companies that hand out **annual dividend raises** like clockwork.

SARAH'S "INFLATION INSURANCE" MOMENT

Sarah, a longtime client and world-class worrier, rang me after reading yet another headline on soaring grocery prices.

"Paul, if inflation keeps running hot, will my dividends keep up—or am I just treading water?"

Instead of launching into theory, I opened her statement and pointed to one of her larger holdings: Procter & Gamble—a company that has increased its dividend every single year since 1957.

"See this line? Last year P&G gave you a 5 percent raise. The year before, 6 percent. They've done that through recessions, wars, and bell-bottoms. When you reinvest those ever-rising payouts, you're buying *more* shares right before the next raise hits. That's inflation insurance with a built-in annual cost-of-living adjustment."

Sarah nodded, finally exhaling. Over the next decade, she watched her P&G stock snowball (not to mention many other positions just like it). Each reinvested dividend bought extra shares, each extra share earned the next year's bigger dividend, and so on. Her income stream didn't just keep pace with inflation—it sprinted ahead, giving her a double-layer shield: compounding plus reliable annual raises.

That's the power combo—reinvest the checks and own companies committed to giving you a raise every year, no begging required.

DIVIDEND GROWTH VERSUS OTHER INFLATION HEDGES

Now, some people might tell you to hedge against inflation with things like gold, real estate, or Treasury Inflation-Protected Securities (TIPS). While those options have their place, they don't offer the same benefits as dividend growth stocks. Here's why.

Gold, for example, doesn't generate income. It just sits there. Sure, it might appreciate in value, but it's not going to send you a check every quarter like dividend stocks do. Plus, gold prices can be volatile, and volatility without income is a very stressful situation for most investors.

Real estate can be a good hedge, but it comes with its own headaches. There's maintenance, tenant issues, illiquidity...and the list goes on. You can't just sell off a portion of your rental property like you can with a stock. However, if you have a great renter, the headaches might be worth it. The right rental property is like a good dividend stock. You can hold an appreciating or depreciating asset but get paid to watch the volatility. Real estate is one of the rare asset classes that act like dividend stocks, but they come with a completely different set of challenges.

TIPS are government bonds that adjust with inflation, but their yields are often low, and they don't offer the growth potential that dividend stocks do.

Dividend growth stocks provide both income and growth. You're getting paid to hold them, and as the company increases its dividend, you're getting more income over time. Plus, if the company's stock price appreciates, you're getting capital gains on top of those dividends. It's a one-two punch that most other inflation hedges can't match.

THE CLIENT WHO WAS WORRIED ABOUT THE "SILENT THIEF"

I had an investor meet with me years ago, Mike, who used to call inflation the "silent thief." He was retired, living off his investments, and every time he noticed the price of gas or groceries go up, he'd rant about how poorly our government was run and how much those bad decisions were costing him (a very familiar frustration I often share).

"Paul, inflation's going to steal my retirement!" he'd say, half joking but mostly serious.

Mike's portfolio was heavily weighted toward bonds, and while bonds can be safe, they weren't giving him the inflation protection he needed.

"Mike," I said, "you need something that's going to grow along with inflation. You should look at adding some dividend growth stocks to your portfolio. These companies are increasing their payouts every year, and that extra cash flow is going to help you keep up with rising prices."

He shifted part of his portfolio into dividend growth stocks—companies with a strong history of increasing their dividends consistently. A few years later, Mike called me with a completely different tone.

"Paul," he said, "I have to tell you, those dividend stocks were the best move I've made. My income's growing, and I don't flinch as much when inflation comes up in the news anymore." He still grumbles about Washington's spending habits every time we meet

("They're printing money like it's Monopoly!"), but now he does it with a smile, because his dividends are outrunning the government's budget deficits one raise at a time.

INFLATION DOESN'T STAND A CHANCE AGAINST DIVIDEND GROWTH

So, what's the big takeaway? Inflation is going to happen. Prices are going to rise, and your purchasing power is going to erode—unless you've got a plan to keep up with it. That's where dividend-growth investing comes in.

By focusing on companies with strong, free cash flow and a history of increasing dividends, you're not just creating a reliable income stream for today—you're creating an income stream that grows over time, protecting your wealth from the effects of inflation. And if you reinvest those dividends, you're compounding that growth, ensuring your future purchasing power stays intact.

Remember Linda, Tom, Sarah, and Mike? They all had different concerns, but they found the same solution: dividend growth. Whether it was Linda's fear of inflation eating into her retirement, Tom's need for growing income, or Mike's worry about the "silent thief," dividend growth stocks provided the protection they needed.

The market might fluctuate, inflation might rise, but your dividend income? That's the one thing you can count on to keep growing, year after year.

On that note, we should talk about taxes. In the next chapter, we'll dive headfirst into the exciting world of tax efficiency and dividend growth. Sounds thrilling, right? Don't worry; I'll make sure it's informative and entertaining as we drill down to the main idea: keeping more of what you earn.

CHAPTER 12

Maximizing Dividends, Minimizing Taxes

Keep Uncle Sam Happy Without Inviting Him to Dinner

Nobody wants to talk about taxes. Just the word "taxes" alone is enough to make you want to brew a cup of chamomile tea and calm your nerves. But here's the thing: When it comes to dividend-growth investing, understanding taxes can be the difference between maximizing your returns and watching Uncle Sam scoop up more of your hard-earned cash than he should. Most investors don't want to hand him any more than necessary.

In this chapter, we'll talk about how dividend-growth investing, when done right, can be one of the most tax-efficient ways to build wealth. Think of it like learning how to drive: once you know the rules of the road, you can navigate with confidence, avoid potholes (taxes), and enjoy the ride (compounding dividends). Don't worry; I'll keep it simple with plenty of stories from my experience to help make sense of it all.

THE IMPORTANCE OF TAX EFFICIENCY IN INVESTING

Let me tell you about my client Dave. Dave loved his dividends, but every year when tax season rolled around, he'd groan. "Paul," he'd say, "I'm getting whacked with taxes! How do I keep more of this money?"

That's when we had the tax-efficiency talk. Tax efficiency is about keeping as much of your investment returns as possible by minimizing the tax bite. And guess what? Dividend-growth investing is like a Swiss Army knife for tax efficiency. With the right strategies, you can grow your wealth and keep more of it.

UNDERSTANDING TAXABLE DIVIDENDS

Let's start with the basics: how dividends are taxed. Dividends come in two flavors: qualified and ordinary. Think of qualified dividends as the VIPs of the tax world. These are taxed at the lower capital gains rate, which is much better than getting taxed at ordinary income rates. Meanwhile, ordinary dividends are taxed like regular income. No one wants that.

The trick is to make sure you're holding onto those dividend-paying stocks long enough to qualify for the lower tax rate. That's right. There's a minimum holding period to ensure your dividends get the qualified treatment. If you've got a solid dividend stock, resist the urge to sell too soon.

To qualify for the lower tax rate on qualified dividends, investors must hold the stock for more than sixty days during the 121-day period that begins sixty days before the ex-dividend date.[17] This roughly translates to a four-month window around the day the company decides who's entitled to the upcoming dividend. By staying

17 Internal Revenue Service, *Investment Income and Expenses (Including Capital Gains and Losses)*, (IRS Pub 550, 2024), https://www.irs.gov/publications/p550.

invested for those sixty-one days, you're showing you're in it for the long haul—not just grabbing a quick dividend and bailing out.

I once had a client, Sarah, who treated her stock account like a TV remote—click, click, click—never staying on one channel long enough to catch the show. "Sarah," I told her, "you're missing out on qualified dividends because you're changing the station too fast (moving in and out of stocks). You're leaving money on the table." Once we tweaked her strategy to give each stock a longer screen time, the tax perks kicked in—and her tax bill slimmed down accordingly.

TAX-DEFERRED ACCOUNTS AND DIVIDEND GROWTH

Now let's explore the magic of tax-deferred accounts, like your traditional 401(k)s and IRAs. When you have these types of accounts, it's like the taxman is giving you a rain check on dividend taxes until you start making withdrawals. It's like delaying a dentist appointment indefinitely—except this time, it's a great idea in a roundabout way.

Here's the beauty: When you reinvest dividends in these tax-deferred accounts, the compounding effect kicks into hyperdrive. You're not losing a chunk of those dividends to Uncle Sam every year, which means more shares, more dividends, and ultimately, more growth. Picture a snowball rolling downhill—it keeps growing bigger and faster, with each dividend adding to the momentum.

Now, to be perfectly honest, I'm not the biggest fan of tax-deferred accounts in the long run, and here's why: When you finally start taking money out, the taxman comes knocking, and you're taxed at your ordinary income rate. It's like finally having that dentist appointment after putting it off for years. You knew it was coming; you just hoped it wouldn't hurt as much.

Still, for the compounding power of dividend growth, tax-deferred accounts play a crucial role in the wealth-building process.

ROTH ACCOUNTS: THE TAX-FREE DIVIDEND GROWTH WONDERLAND

Now, if tax-deferred accounts are good, Roth IRAs are the absolute best—like winning the tax lottery. Why? Because a Roth IRA is a tax-free growth machine. Here's how it works: You contribute after-tax dollars today, and once that money is inside your Roth, everything—capital gains, dividends, you name it—grows tax free. When you finally withdraw the money in retirement, you won't owe a single penny in taxes. All growth, all dividends, everything is completely tax free.

Imagine reinvesting your dividends inside a Roth: You're compounding those earnings year after year without ever worrying about the taxman coming to take a slice of your pie. It's like planting a money tree that keeps growing, and when it's time to harvest, you keep everything. You don't even have to share the fruit.

If you're looking to supercharge your dividend growth strategy and maximize your after-tax returns, the Roth IRA is where you want to be. While tax-deferred accounts are great for compounding, nothing beats the peace of mind that comes with tax-free growth in a Roth.

TAX-LOSS HARVESTING AND DIVIDEND GROWTH

Here's a fun strategy that turns lemons into lemonade: tax-loss harvesting. Now, nobody likes losing money in the market, but what if I told you those losses could help you reduce your tax bill?

Here's how it works: Let's say you've got a stock that's gone south, and you're sitting on a loss. You can sell that stock, use the loss to offset some of your dividend gains (or other gains), and reduce your taxable income. Then, after thirty days (to avoid the "wash sale" rule), you can even buy the stock back if you still believe in it.

I had a client, Mike, who had a stock that just wasn't performing. "Paul," he said, "I hate to sell it at a loss, but what can I do?"

"Mike," I told him, "let's use that loss to our advantage." We sold the stock, offset his dividend gains, and thirty days later, he bought it back at a lower price. Not only did he reduce his tax bill, but he also got the stock cheaper! That's tax-loss harvesting in action.

DIVIDENDS VERSUS CAPITAL GAINS: A TAX COMPARISON

Market timing is that mythical skill we all secretly think we have—right up until we buy, the stock drops, we sell, and it pops the next morning. It's like trying to pick the fastest checkout lane at the grocery store: Whichever line you choose instantly becomes the one with the price check on canned beans. Dividends sidestep that headache because you don't have to guess *when* the payoff arrives; it shows up automatically, and—if it's a qualified dividend—at a gentler tax rate. Capital gains? Valuable, yes, but you only pocket them when you sell, and choosing that moment without a crystal ball can feel like playing darts in the dark.

Enter my client John—an unapologetic growth chaser. "Paul, I just want this portfolio to *rocket*," he told me. (Honestly, who doesn't? We'd all love our statements to look like Jack's beanstalk.) But betting only on price appreciation is like stretching a giant rubber band: thrilling while it's taut, nerve-racking if it snaps back.

So I suggested a hybrid approach: keep hunting for growth, but add high-quality dividend growers—especially when they're temporarily on sale. Buying a dependable, free cash-flow machine at a discount is like winding a spring toy: It might sit still for a bit, but when the market mood shifts, it lurches forward *and* pays you for the wait.

That's the sweet spot—capital gains potential *plus* a steady dividend stream. Now John still checks his quotes for those exhilarating upticks, but he also smiles every quarter when the dividend deposits hit—no dart throwing required.

HOLDING PERIODS AND TAX EFFICIENCY

Another key to tax efficiency is understanding holding periods. The longer you hold your dividend stocks, the more tax-efficient your portfolio becomes. If you sell too soon, you may end up paying short-term capital gains taxes, which are much higher than long-term capital gains taxes. Plus, you'll miss out on a qualified dividend tax treatment.

Let's circle back to Sarah from earlier, who loved jumping in and out of stocks. Once she held her stocks for longer periods, she not only reduced her taxes, but she also saw her overall returns improve. That's because she wasn't paying short-term capital gains taxes, and her dividends were getting the qualified treatment.

DIVIDEND REINVESTMENT PLANS (DRIPS) AND TAXES

If you're like many dividend investors, you might be using a dividend reinvestment plan (DRIP). DRIPs are a great way to automatically reinvest your dividends, buying more shares without having to think about it. But here's a little-known fact: Even though you're reinvesting, those dividends are still taxable in a regular brokerage account.

I had a client, Linda, who loved her DRIP. "Paul," she said, "I'm reinvesting every dividend, but why do I have to pay taxes on dividend reinvestments?"

I explained that, unfortunately, the IRS still wants its cut, even if you're not pocketing the cash. We set up a system to keep track of her cost basis, and Linda minimized the tax impact when she eventually sold her shares.

MANAGING TAXES IN RETIREMENT

Taxes don't stop when you retire. In fact, they can become even more important. If you're relying on dividends for income in retirement, you'll want to be strategic about how you manage your withdrawals from tax-deferred accounts like IRAs.

Let me tell you about my client Mark. Mark was about to retire, and he had a mix of taxable accounts and tax-deferred accounts (IRAs). "Paul," he asked, "how do I take money out without getting crushed by taxes?"

We worked out a plan where Mark could withdraw from his taxable accounts first, taking advantage of the lower taxes on qualified dividends. By holding off on his IRA withdrawals, we reduced his overall tax burden in retirement.

Though this strategy worked well for Mark, it's important to remember that every retirement tax plan should be tailored to the individual. For some retirees, it might make sense to take withdrawals from tax-deferred accounts like IRAs earlier, especially while tax rates are relatively low.

Waiting too long can lead to higher taxes down the road when required minimum distributions (RMDs) kick in, or if tax laws change, which could make withdrawals far more expensive in the future. The key is to evaluate your situation, project your future income needs, and work with a professional to create a tax strategy that minimizes your burden while maximizing your retirement income. Every situation is unique, and there's no one-size-fits-all solution.

CREATING A TAX-EFFICIENT DIVIDEND GROWTH PORTFOLIO

Now, let's discuss building a tax-efficient portfolio. The key is to use a mix of tax-deferred accounts, qualified dividends, and long-term holdings to minimize your tax bill and maximize your returns.

One of the best strategies I've seen is using high-dividend stocks in tax-advantaged accounts, like IRAs, and holding growth-oriented dividend stocks in taxable accounts to take advantage of qualified dividends. This approach helps you grow wealth without constantly worrying about the taxman knocking on your door.

THE POWER OF TAX EFFICIENCY IN LONG-TERM WEALTH BUILDING

What's the bottom line? When it comes to dividend-growth investing, tax efficiency is one of the most powerful tools in your arsenal. By understanding how dividends are taxed, using tax-deferred accounts, and employing strategies like tax-loss harvesting, you can maximize your after-tax returns and build wealth faster.

Here's the kicker: Understanding taxes doesn't just save you money—it also reduces the stress and anxiety that comes with investing. When your investments are set up to minimize taxes, you can focus on the long term and let time, compounding, and your dividends grow your money.

Now that we've taken a deep dive into managing taxes like a pro, it's time to talk about the magic of total return. We'll explore that in the next chapter, along with how combining capital appreciation and dividend income can be the secret recipe for long-term financial success.

CHAPTER 13

Dividends + Growth = Total Return

Getting Paid to Eat Your Pizza and Save a Slice for Later

Picture this: You're at your favorite pizzeria, ready to dig into the largest pie they've got. You have two options. One: You can focus entirely on how many slices of pizza you can devour right now, making sure you get as much as possible before your friends swoop in. Or two: You could pace yourself, enjoy each slice, and, better yet, stash a few slices in the fridge for tomorrow. (Let's be honest—leftover pizza is one of God's little gifts to us.)

This brings us to the concept of total return in investing. You see, some investors are like the first pizza-eater—obsessed with short-term gains, or in investing terms, capital appreciation. They're focused on how much the stock price can rise, how fast they can get in and out, and how quickly they can make a buck.

Then there's the second type: the dividend investor who's looking at the entire picture. They're not just focused on how much their stock will go up (although that's nice); they're also thinking about the income the stock will generate for years to come.

This is where total return comes in: It's the combination of capital appreciation (the rise in stock price) and dividend income (the slices you stash for later). And when you understand how these two work together, you'll see why dividend-growth investing is the ultimate long-term strategy.

Let's dig into how total return works and why it matters, and, of course, I'll share stories from my career to help make sense of it all.

TOTAL RETURN: THE WHOLE PIZZA

Total return is the sum of capital appreciation and dividend income. What are they? In a nutshell:

1. **Capital Appreciation:** This is the part most people focus on. It's the rise in the value of your stock over time. You bought it at fifty dollars, and now it's worth seventy-five dollars—that's capital appreciation.
2. **Dividend Income:** This is the cash the company pays you just for owning its stock. If you own dividend-paying stocks, these payments come in regularly, like clockwork, regardless of what the stock price is doing.

To put it simply, total return is the growth in the stock's price plus the dividends you've received. It's the entire pizza. While everyone else is obsessing over whether their stock has gone up 5 percent or 10 percent, you're quietly collecting dividend checks and watching your total return grow over time.

WHY CHASING CAPITAL GAINS ALONE DOESN'T WORK

Let's address the elephant in the room: why focusing solely on capital gains doesn't always work for long-term investors. It's like trying to win a marathon by sprinting the first mile—you might feel great at first, but there's a good chance you'll be dragging yourself across the finish line (if you make it at all).

I had a friend named Steve, a real go-getter. He was all about high-growth stocks. The guy loved the thrill of watching his stock prices jump 20 percent in a week, though it didn't happen much. The problem: When the market tanked, those high-growth stocks didn't just dip, they plummeted. Steve's portfolio was like a roller coaster: great on the way up, but terrifying on the way down.

"Paul," Steve said to me, "I can't take these swings anymore. Every time I think I've made it, the market wipes out my gains."

I explained to Steve that chasing capital gains alone is a risky game. It's unpredictable. You're putting all your chips on stock price appreciation, which is not only volatile but often out of your control. The market has a mind of its own, and even the best stocks can get dragged down when things turn ugly.

This is where dividend growth comes in. I told Steve, "You want to smooth out those wild swings? Add some dividend growth stocks to your portfolio."

Dividend-paying companies don't just rely on market movements to create value. They provide consistent income in the form of dividends, which means even when the market goes through rough patches, you're still getting paid. Over time, these companies tend to appreciate in value as well, providing that capital growth Steve was after—without the nausea-inducing roller-coaster ride.

By focusing on total return, Steve could enjoy the upside of capital gains and the steady cash flow from dividends. Suddenly, his portfolio wasn't such a wild ride anymore.

DIVIDEND GROWTH AS THE FOUNDATION OF TOTAL RETURN

Here's something a lot of investors overlook: Dividends aren't just about providing you with a nice quarterly check—they're a key component of total return. When you reinvest your dividends, you're effectively adding fuel to the total return fire, compounding your returns over time.

Let's revisit Karen from earlier. Once she started reinvesting her dividends, her portfolio didn't just grow—it accelerated. Her dividends bought more shares, which generated more dividends. It's the classic snowball effect, and it's one of the most powerful forces in the investing world.

Here's something to keep in mind: Not all dividends are created equal. Some companies pay high dividends but never increase them. That's fine for a while, but over time, inflation will eat away at the value of those static payments. What you want are dividend growth stocks—companies that not only pay dividends but consistently raise them.

This is why companies like Procter & Gamble, Johnson & Johnson, and Coca-Cola have been investor favorites for decades. These are companies with a proven track record of increasing their dividends year after year. They generate strong free cash flow, which means they reward shareholders while growing their business.

Dividend growth isn't just about income, but about creating growing income. When you combine that with capital appreciation, you're looking at the foundation of a strong total return strategy. Over time, those growing dividends make a huge difference in your portfolio's overall value.

THE CLIENT WHO WANTED ONLY CAPITAL GAINS

Let me tell you about an investor we'll call Jake. He breezed into my office, waving his phone like a victory flag, a year-to-date chart of some rocket-ship tech stock glowing on the screen. "Paul," he said, half-laughing, half buzzing on adrenaline, "if the price keeps doing *that*, who needs dividends? Those are for retirees and envelope stuffers. I'm here for rocket growth."

Jake wasn't alone. A whole group of investors out there gets fixated on stock growth, like they're betting on a horse race. Here's what I told him: "Jake, you're missing half the pizza. You're so focused on capital appreciation that you're ignoring the steady income dividends bring in. Those dividends keep your portfolio growing, even when the market decides to take a nap."

He was skeptical, so I ran some numbers for him. We looked at two companies: one that had been paying dividends for years and steadily increasing them, and another that was purely focused on growth. Over a decade, the dividend-paying stock's total return was higher—not just because the stock price increased but because Jake would have been receiving dividend income that he could reinvest for compounding growth. And reinvesting those dividends is like adding extra toppings to your pizza without paying extra.

By the end of our conversation, Jake saw the light. He realized dividends weren't just a nice little bonus—they were a key part of total return. And as someone who loves numbers, he was thrilled to see how those "small" dividend payments could add up to a massive boost in his portfolio, though he still likes to chase those gains.

THE POWER OF COMPOUNDING: REINVESTING YOUR DIVIDENDS

Let's take Jake's story a little further and talk about compounding. If you're not reinvesting your dividends, it's like leaving money on the table—or, worse, like throwing away perfectly good slices of pizza because you're "full" at the moment. Trust me, you'll want those slices later.

Reinvesting dividends is one of the most powerful tools in the world of investing. Reinvesting your dividends buys you more shares of the stock, so you receive even more dividends the next time they're paid. It's a cycle of compounding growth.

Here's how I explained it to another client, Karen, from earlier. (And no, she isn't a Karen; that's just her name.) Karen was in her mid-forties and just starting to think seriously about her retirement strategy. She had a nice portfolio of dividend-paying stocks, but she wasn't reinvesting her dividends.

"Karen," I said, "you're doing great collecting those dividend checks, but if you reinvest them, you will supercharge your total return. Think of it like this: Each dividend you reinvest is a seed from the tree you've already grown. When you plant that seed, it grows into another tree, which eventually bears even more fruit. Before you know it, you'll have an orchard full of trees, all producing fruit, and that's how your income keeps multiplying over time."

I showed Karen how reinvesting dividends could take her portfolio to the next level. We crunched the numbers, and over twenty years, the difference between reinvesting and not reinvesting was staggering. By reinvesting, she wasn't just growing her capital—she was growing her income stream, which would make her retirement even more comfortable.

Karen reinvested her dividends immediately, and now she's watching her portfolio grow into an orchard. Just remember, even though you're letting those dividends blossom on their own, Uncle Sam still wants a piece of that harvest. If you need a quick refresher on how taxes might nibble at your DRIP's bounty, jump back to the "Dividend Reinvestment Plans (DRIPs) and Taxes" section in Chapter 12.

MAKE CAPITAL APPRECIATION AND DIVIDENDS WORK TOGETHER

Plenty of investors assume they have to pick a lane—either chase racy capital gains or collect grandma-style dividends. Spoiler: You can absolutely have both, and you don't need to knit doilies to enjoy it.

Enter Bill, a growth-stock true believer. He plopped into my office chair, clutching a printout of a tech darling's five-year chart—basically a hockey stick on caffeine.

"Paul," he said, "this is how I hit my beach-house number. Dividend stocks are like watching paint dry."

I slid over two fresh charts. One showed the same growth rocket he loved; the other showed a dividend grower that looked tame—until you added up the quarterly payouts.

"Bill," I said, "your growth pick is the hare—sprints ahead, but every market pothole knocks it on its fuzzy tail. This dividend stock is a tortoise...with a jet pack full of quarterly checks."

He raised an eyebrow, so we ran the math:

- Ten years of steady price gains plus reinvested dividends equals total return that not only caught the hare but passed it when the market hit a speed bump.
- Smaller drawdowns in the ugly years—because companies with fat free-cash-flow cushions don't panic-slash like fad stocks do.

"Think Microsoft, Apple—boring? Hardly," I said. "They mail you money every quarter and still have enough cash to invent the next big thing."

Bill laughed. "So you're saying I can own a rocket ship that hands me snacks during the flight?"

"Exactly. And when turbulence hits, it doesn't dump you out the hatch."

He swapped a chunk of his all-growth lineup for dividend growers with real balance-sheet muscle. Now, when the market gyrates, his portfolio still climbs—but it also tosses him a paycheck. Bill finally realized the smartest ride to the beach house is the one that keeps moving forward and hands you piña-colada money along the way.

THE DIVIDEND YIELD TRAP: WHY HIGH YIELDS AREN'T ALWAYS BETTER

Let's shift gears for a second and talk about something that trips up a lot of investors: dividend yield. I've already talked about it, but let's review. Dividend yield is just the annual dividend payment divided by the stock price. So if a stock pays a two-dollar dividend, and the stock is fifty dollars, that's a 4 percent yield. Simple enough, right? But here's the thing: A high yield isn't always a good thing. In fact, it can sometimes be a big red flag.

I had a client named Laura who came to me with a stock she was excited about. "Paul, this company has a dividend yield of 8 percent! Isn't that amazing?"

Eight percent *looked* amazing—until I looked under the hood. The company was struggling. Their stock price had dropped significantly, which made the yield look artificially high. And while they were still paying that dividend, it was clear they couldn't sustain it for much longer.

"Laura," I said, "a high yield is great, but only if the company can afford to keep paying it. If their free cash flow can't support that dividend, they will have to cut it. When that happens, the stock price will probably take a hit too."

Sure enough, a little more than a year later, that company cut its dividend, and the stock price continued to tank. Laura was glad she hadn't taken the leap to invest in that company.

The moral of the story? Don't chase yield. Prioritize companies with a history of dividend increases and strong free cash flow. A steady, growing dividend is always better than a high dividend that's on shaky ground.

TOTAL RETURN IN BEAR MARKETS: THE SAFETY NET OF DIVIDENDS

One of the sweetest perks of dividend-growth investing is how it behaves when Mr. Market throws a tantrum. Share prices may slip and slide, but the dividend checks keep showing up—like having an umbrella in a downpour. You'll still get damp, but you won't look like a drowned cat.

Back in the post-'08 rubble, a prospective client named Mark shuffled into my office clutching a brokerage statement from his "diversified" mutual-fund lineup—down nearly 40 percent. "Paul," he groaned, "I'm bleeding money every day. There has to be a better way than watching my funds melt."

Mark's portfolio was the classic Wall Street stew: sprawling mutual funds that rose with the tide but offered zero comfort when the water vanished. I pulled up a sample of dividend-growth companies—firms with fat free-cash-flow cushions that had just raised their payouts while everyone else was hoarding paper clips.

"See these payments?" I said. "They didn't skip a beat during the crash—and they'll buy you more shares at fire-sale prices while you wait for the rebound."

Skeptical but intrigued, Mark shifted a chunk of his mutual-fund holdings into a basket of dividend raisers. Fast-forward to the pandemic sell-off of 2020: the market was doing cartwheels again, and Mark shot me a one-line email:

"Price is ugly, checks are lovely. Sleeping fine. Thanks."

When the dust settled, his new dividend portfolio had recovered faster *and* kept the income spigot wide open the entire time. That's total return in real life: capital gains plus a reliable paycheck—rain, shine, or full-blown bear.

THE TAX ADVANTAGE OF DIVIDENDS

Let's talk about taxes again. Everyone's favorite topic, right? Dividends come with a hidden bonus: tax efficiency, which I touched upon in Chapter 12. But did you know most countries' tax dividends are at a lower rate than ordinary income, especially if they're qualified dividends? That's like getting paid extra just because the government is cutting you some slack.

I'm not saying you should build your entire investment strategy around taxes, because that's a surefire way to drive yourself nuts. However, it's definitely worth considering.

If you're receiving dividend income, especially from qualified dividends, you're not getting hit as hard as you would be if that income came from a paycheck or from selling stock.

I had a client, Don, who was always concerned about taxes. "Paul," he said, "I hate paying Uncle Sam a portion of my income. How can I keep more of my money?"

I explained that dividend-growth investing offers a tax-efficient way to generate income. "Don," I told him, "those dividends you're getting are taxed at a lower rate than your regular income. If you hold on to your shares for the long term, you're only paying capital gains taxes when you sell—which is also taxed lower than ordinary income."

For Don, that was a game changer. He realized by focusing on dividend growth, he could grow his wealth and keep more of it.

MAMBA MENTALITY MEETS DIVIDEND INVESTING

Remember all the way back in Chapter 1, how I kicked things off with basketball? I asked your opinion about MJ, LeBron, and some guy named Kobe. Then I went ahead and wrote about the first two, but promised to bring Kobe back. I was waiting patiently, like a black mamba in the grass ready to strike. Now's the time.

Let me tell you, if you never got the chance to see Kobe Bryant in action, you missed out on a performance that often felt more like a live-action superhero movie than a basketball game. I'll never forget watching him drop sixty points in a single outing.[18] Every bucket looked like a clinic, and the poor defenders might as well have been folding chairs for all the good they did. The man's eyes had that laser focus, and when the Black Mamba locked onto a target, even the sound of the buzzer wouldn't break his trance.

Of course, we all know Kobe's greatness sprang from what he famously called the "Mamba Mentality."[19] It wasn't just talent; it was an unrelenting commitment to excellence: endless hours in the gym, an obsessive attention to detail, and a mindset that screamed, "I'm doing whatever it takes to win." What set him apart was he never coasted. Whether it was the first minute or the final seconds, you knew Kobe would put in 110 percent like a thoroughbred refusing to slow down at the finish line.

As for the link between Kobe and the world of dividends, I want you to picture a handful of blue-chip companies that treat their dividend payouts the same way Kobe treated basketball. They have that same unyielding drive to "win," which for them means paying (and often raising) dividends year after year—rain or shine, recession or not. It's no accident these companies are called Dividend Aristocrats. These are the companies, like Kobe, that show up ready to work harder than everyone else in the room.

They slash expenses, pivot strategies, even trim other projects, all in service of one goal: to keep that dividend train rolling. Much like watching Kobe nailing a game-winning fadeaway, these companies keep delivering, quarter after quarter, fueled by a Mamba-like refusal to let investors down.

---

18 National Basketball Association, "This Date in History—Kobe Bryant Scores 60 Points in His Final NBA Game (4/13/16)," NBA.com, accessed August 6, 2025, https://www.nba.com/watch/video/this-date-in-history-kobe-bryant-scores-60-points-in-his-final-nba-game-4-13-16.

19 Kobe Bryant, *The Mamba Mentality* (MCD, 2018).

When you think about resilience, consistency, and sheer willpower in investing, remember Kobe's Mamba Mentality—because some companies bring that same unstoppable energy to their dividend payouts. And that, my friend, is the magic of investing in a team that simply refuses to lose.

WHY TOTAL RETURN IS THE ULTIMATE MEASURE OF SUCCESS

What have we learned about total return? From my perspective, when it comes to investing, focusing on total return is like having your cake and eating it too (or pizza, which we've been eating since the start of the chapter).

You're not just relying on the stock price to go up. You're also cashing in on dividend income, which provides a steady stream of cash flow that can keep growing over time.

By focusing on dividend growth, you're setting yourself up for success in both bull and bear markets. You're not chasing quick gains, but instead, you're building a portfolio that will grow consistently and reliably, year after year.

Whether you're reinvesting those dividends or using them for income, the combination of capital appreciation and dividend growth is what will help you build long-term wealth. It's not about getting rich quick—it's about getting rich *for sure.*

Remember, total return is the whole pizza, and dividend growth is the cheese that holds it all together. So, focus on the companies committed to growing their dividends, and let your capital and your income work in harmony to create a rock-solid investment strategy.

Okay, now for my next question: How can you stay cool when the market tries to set your hair on fire? If that sounds like a topic for a whole other chapter—you're right. We're about to leave our spreadsheets and stock tickers behind and dive into the most unpredictable part of investing: *your own mind.*

(Go easy on that pizza. This might be a bit of a roller-coaster ride.)

CHAPTER 14

The Psychology of Dividend Growth

Keep Calm and Let Your Dividends Do the Work

Let's be real—when it comes to investing, most of the battles we face are not market related but in our heads. Our emotions love to turn up the heat when stocks start to dip or when the media says the next big crash is just around the corner. Fear, greed, panic, and excitement—they're all sitting front row, shouting advice we know we shouldn't take. But here's the thing: Mastering the psychology of investing is everything—especially in dividend-growth investing, where the rewards come not to the swift, but to the steady and disciplined.

In this chapter, we'll dive into the behavioral side of dividend-growth investing and why keeping your cool is often more important than knowing the latest stock trend. I'll share stories from my career, sprinkle in a few lessons from behavioral finance, and give you strategies for becoming the investor who can calmly weather any storm.

THE BEHAVIORAL PITFALLS OF INVESTING: WHY OUR MINDS MESS WITH US

Let's start with a quick trip inside the mind of a typical investor—maybe like my fellow advisor, Tyler. He loved investing, but he had one Achilles' heel. Every time the market had a good day, Tyler thought he was a genius. And every time the market had a bad day, he was ready to cash out and buy a cabin in the woods.

"Paul,"Tyler said, "why does investing feel like an emotional roller coaster?"

Here's the deal: Humans aren't wired for rational investing. We're wired for survival, and when it feels like the sky is falling, our instinct is to *run*. But running during a market downturn often means locking in losses. Then there's greed. When the market's soaring, greed whispers, "This time it's different! Keep buying! Don't miss out!"

Tyler's experience is a classic case of the two emotional villains in investing: **fear** and **greed**. These emotions push people to buy when prices are high and sell when they're low, the exact opposite of what we should be doing. And don't get me started on overconfidence. That's when you think you're the next Warren Buffett, but really, you're just riding a market wave that's bound to crash.

HOW DIVIDEND GROWTH INVESTING KEEPS YOU GROUNDED

Here's why dividend-growth investing is the antidote to market hysteria: When you measure your scoreboard in *deposits* rather than *quotes*, a down day feels more like a coupon than a crisis. The only questions that matter are, "Will this company keep paying me?" and "Will that paycheck get bigger?"

Take Sarah, a longtime client who'd built up a solid mix of dividend raisers. About three months into the 2020 slide, after the headlines had hammered home all the bad news, I rang her just to make sure the nightly doomscroll hadn't rattled her nerves.

Me: "Hey, Sarah, it's Paul. How are you feeling about the portfolio with everything still pretty bumpy out there?"

Sarah: "Honestly, I was going to call you. Prices keep slipping and I've got some cash sitting in savings. Should I be nervous, or is this a good time to put that money to work?"

Me: "First things first. Are those quarterly dividend deposits still hitting your checking account?"

Sarah: "Yep, just saw another one last week."

Me: "Perfect. Do you remember the companies we picked? They've raised their payouts every year for more than a decade. The latest earnings showed they still cover the dividend with plenty of room. So nothing in the income story has changed except the sticker price."

Sarah: "So if I buy now, I'm basically getting a bigger dividend on a stock I already own?"

Me: "Exactly. You're buying the same cash-flow machine, just only on sale. Think of it like getting your favorite brand of coffee at half price: same caffeine, better deal."

Sarah: "All right, let's load the cart."

Sarah didn't need to predict the market's bottom. She just needed reassurance that the dividend engine was still purring. With that confirmed, the lower prices looked less like danger and more like a coupon—one that would keep paying her every quarter and likely hike those payments next year too. That's a client who "gets it." When your portfolio is built on reliable, growing cash flow, the real panic isn't a downturn—it's missing the sale.

EMOTIONAL DISCIPLINE: KEEP YOUR COOL WHEN THE HEAT'S ON

Market volatility isn't just a stress test for your portfolio. It's a pop quiz on patience, and most of us crammed for that subject about as well as we did for high-school calculus.

Take my buddy Kevin. Smart guy, loyal scarlet-and-gray Buckeye (he still starts sentences with "O-H!" even when no one answers "I-O"). I'm a Michigan fan—yes, the last four rivalry games had me strutting like I invented football—which means our annual November trash talk is practically a contact sport.

Kevin loves dissecting stock charts over wings and college highlights, but the minute the market hiccups he texts:

"Dude, do I mash the sell button now and buy back in after the dust settles?"

After the fourth midnight alert, I finally replied, "Kev, you're not investing for the next quarter—you're investing for the next quarter century." He shot back that I've been saying "just be patient" almost as often as I've reminded him of the scoreboard (guilty on both counts), but the line stuck.

The point? Volatility is inevitable; abandoning a solid plan every time a headline shouts is optional. Dividends make discipline easier. Those quarterly deposits keep rolling in—even when prices bounce around like a toddler on a trampoline. You've got something tangible anchoring your sanity. Progress continues, drama or no drama, and Kevin can save the panic-button mashing for the next time the Wolverines visit Columbus.

PATIENCE IS KEY, AND DIVIDEND GROWTH REWARDS THE PATIENT

Patience is a lot easier to talk about than to practice. We live in a world that's all about quick wins, but dividend-growth investing is the opposite of that. It's the tortoise in the tortoise versus hare race.

I had a client, John, who came to me frustrated. "Paul, I've been reinvesting dividends for two years, and I'm not seeing any huge returns. Should I switch strategies?"

I told him a little secret. "John, you're in the slow-cooker game. Dividend-growth investing isn't about getting rich quick. It's about getting rich for sure—over time. Take Warren Buffett, for example. Did you know 99 percent of his wealth was earned after his fiftieth birthday?[20] If Buffett had started investing in his fifties instead of his teens, he'd have barely made a dent in his current fortune—around eleven million by age sixty instead of the eighty-one billion he actually had. It wasn't the stock picks that made him wealthy. **It was time.**"

When you reinvest your dividends, something magical happens. You get more shares, which pay more dividends, which buy more shares, which pay even more dividends. It's the ultimate compounding effect. But here's the catch: It takes time. Those who have the patience to let it work its magic are rewarded in the end.

OVERCOMING SHORT-TERM THINKING: WHY THE MARKET ISN'T YOUR FRIEND

Here's a hard truth: The market is not your friend, at least not in the short term. The market loves to lure you into short-term thinking with flashy headlines and big price swings. But if you're focused on dividends, you don't need to play that game.

---

20 Morgan Housel, *The Psychology of Money: Timeless Lessons on Wealth, Greed, and Happiness* (Harriman House, 2020).

Let me tell you about my client Mike. Mike was a smart guy, but like a lot of people, he got caught up in the hype of quick gains. "Paul, I heard this stock is about to blow up. Should we buy in?"

I took a deep breath and said, "Mike, I'm not in the business of betting. You're not here for fireworks. You're here to build a long-term strategy, right?"

"Right," he sighed.

Dividend-growth investing forces you to take the long view. When you're focused on building an income stream over decades, the daily market noise becomes just that—noise. The more you focus on dividends, the less tempted you'll be to chase the next big thing.

THE PSYCHOLOGICAL BENEFITS OF CONSISTENT INCOME: KEEP CALM AND COLLECT DIVIDENDS

Here's the psychological beauty of dividend growth: It gives you consistency in a world that often feels anything but consistent. When stock prices are bouncing up and down, those steady dividend checks provide peace of mind. It's like having a paycheck you can count on, even if your boss (the market) is being a little unpredictable.

I once had a client, Mark, who called me during the market meltdown of 2008. "Paul, everything's down—should I sell?"

I asked him, "Is your rent still getting paid?"

He laughed. "Of course, but what does that have to do with anything?"

I said, "Your dividends are like your rent. Even if your property value dips, you're still getting paid every month. That's how dividends work too. Your stocks may be down, but you're still getting your paychecks."

Mark didn't sell, and sure enough, his dividends kept rolling in. The market eventually recovered, and Mark was sitting in a much better place with even more income and greater value in his portfolio.

BUILDING EMOTIONAL RESILIENCE FOR MARKET VOLATILITY: STAY THE COURSE

The final piece of dividend-growth psychology is emotional resilience. It's simple in theory but tricky in practice. Headlines howl, prices lurch, and that bright-red *SELL* button can begin looking like a lifeboat.

Take Steve, a brand-new client who'd been with us barely three months when the market threw its first tantrum. His welcome-to-volatility call came in hot: "Paul, I knew stocks moved around, but this feels like a carnival ride gone wrong."

We pressed pause and walked through his plan. Long-term goals? Check. Dividend income already hitting his account? Check. The companies' histories of raising those payouts? Double-check.

"Steve," I said, "think of the market like working for a cranky boss. Some days are brutal, but the paycheck shows up every two weeks whether he's slamming doors or handing out donuts. Your dividends are that paycheck. Walk out now, and you fire yourself from the income you hired these companies to produce."

He took a breath, stayed put, and a month later sent a short email: *"Boss still grumpy—paycheck still clears. Feeling better."* That's emotional resilience in action: a nervous newcomer learning that dividends keep clocking in, even when Mr. Market calls in sick.

LET TIME DO THE HEAVY LIFTING

Dividend-growth investing isn't just about picking the right stocks. It's about mastering your emotions and sticking with a long-term plan, no matter how tempting it is to panic or chase shiny objects along the way.

It's like being in a marathon. You're not sprinting for quick gains; you're pacing yourself for the long haul. The market may have mood swings, but your dividends? They're like the steady paycheck that shows up whether the boss is smiling or slamming doors.

Epilogue

Together, you and I have explored the ins and outs of dividend-growth investing, the psychology of investing, and the realities of stock-market benchmarks, and hopefully we had a few laughs along the way. You've armed yourself with the knowledge to build a solid, income-generating portfolio that fits your unique financial needs and goals. But this journey doesn't end here—it's just beginning.

As Paul Harvey wisely put it, "In times like these, it's helpful to remember that there have always been times like these. The stock market is a roller coaster. It's only those who jump off who get hurt."

Here's the key to making it through whatever the market throws your way: Stay buckled in. You have to ride the ups and downs, because in the long run, the market always recovers. It's the people who panic and jump off that end up losing the most.

I believe there's real magic in dividend-growth investing—a magic that isn't about timing the market but time itself.

You're building something that compounds, grows, and gives back to you, year after year. When you stay the course, keep your emotions in check, and focus on the big picture, you win the game—not by luck, but by practice, patience, and discipline.

Will the market throw another tantrum? Yes—it always does (maybe it's happening right now as you read this). What can you do? Here are some ideas:

- Take a deep breath.
- Grab a coffee.
- Have another slice of pizza.
- Remind yourself you're not here to get rich quick.

That's right. You're here to get rich for sure. And your dividends? They're the best coworkers you've ever had. They'll keep showing up, even when the market feels like it's ready to quit.

Most importantly, you don't have to do this alone. Every great journey is made stronger with the right support. If, at any point, you feel uncertain or overwhelmed, don't hesitate to raise your hand and ask for help.

Whether it's a trusted financial advisor, a mentor, or the tools we've introduced along the way, you're never truly alone in this process. There's power in seeking guidance when you need it, and sometimes, the smartest move you can make is knowing when to ask for assistance.

As you take these next steps toward financial independence and a more secure future, know this: You're equipped with the tools and strategies to take control of your income and your investments. You've learned how to navigate the noise of the markets, measure what truly matters, and create a plan that's uniquely yours.

Now, it's time to act. Your financial future is in your hands.

So, go forward boldly. This is your journey, and you're the architect of your success. The road ahead is yours to shape, and while the markets may rise and fall, your path is clear. Stick to your plan, stay true to your goals, and remember you have everything you need to create the future you've always dreamed of.

Here's to your success, your freedom, and your future. You've got this.

Acknowledgments

(This section of the book is where I thank everyone who kept me from turning this manuscript into a four-hundred-page rant about inflation.)

First, to **my wife, Stephanie**—the real CFO of our household. You endured more "Honey, listen to this dividend stat!" monologues than any human should, yet you still saved me a seat on the couch. Your patience, endless efforts, and strategic food deliveries turned late-night scribbles into readable sentences. I love you more than compound interest (and you know how I feel about compound interest).

To **Evan, Shane, and Reid**—thanks for letting Dad test-drive metaphors at the dinner table. If you can explain free cash flow to a fourteen-year-old, you can explain it to *anyone*. Someday you'll appreciate the head start on your own dividend portfolios (even if the allowance-matching program was a hard sell).

Mom and Dad—you modeled thrift, generosity, and the kind of work ethic that would make the Black Mamba proud. You taught me to leave every campsite—and balance sheet—better than I found it.

The Hot-Tub Crew in San Diego—especially the friend who uttered the fateful line, "Dividends are the unsung heroes." Without that splash of humility, I'd still be timing the market instead of writing about patience. The next round of room-temperature networking is on me.

My **Insight Folios** and **Uplift Technology** team—you took a half-baked Excel sheet and built real software that helps real people sleep at night. Thanks for turning nerdy math into something beautiful (and for QA testing every example in this book).

Compliance—thanks for letting me keep the jokes that *barely* cleared the bar. Your red ink saved me from at least three career-limiting footnotes.

To my **early readers and eagle-eyed editors, Mark, Dave, and others**—consider this your official dividend: a lifetime exemption from any future drafts with missing citations.

Finally, a nod to **Michael, Kobe, and LeBron** for the endless on-court metaphors, and to the University of Michigan football team for giving me four straight years of material to needle my Buckeye friends. That rivalry—like the market—reminds me to enjoy the ride, respect the cycles, and always keep a sense of humor.

If this book helps even one reader turn financial anxiety into financial freedom, the credit belongs to everyone above. Any remaining typos, bad dad jokes, or questionable pizza analogies are 100 percent mine.

Thank you all for believing, encouraging, and occasionally proofreading under duress. Now let's get back to letting our money work while we don't have to.

About the Author

PAUL DURSO is the president of Uplift Technologies and founder of Insight Folios—two Charlotte-based outfits that prove spreadsheets can be exciting. He also created *Planning Made Simple* to help advisors and investors understand money without needing a translator or a pot of coffee the size of a hockey helmet.

When Paul isn't decoding dividends on CBS or FOX, you'll find him attempting to keep up with three turbocharged sons—Evan, Shane, and Reid—while his far-more-patient wife, Stephanie, reminds him that golf balls all over the house do NOT count as modern art.

A Certified Estate Planner, Certified Wealth Strategist, and Certified Retirement Planner (he collects credentials the way kids collect trading cards), Paul still insists his greatest titles are **Husband, Dad, and Follower of Jesus.** He believes faith comes first, family is priceless, and compound interest is proof God wants us to plan ahead.

Made in the USA
Monee, IL
13 September 2026

62979110R00100